Handbook
of
Counseling
Supervision

Handbook
of
Counseling
Supervision

L. DiAnne Borders
Oakland University
and
George R. Leddick
Indiana-Purdue University

Contributors

Janine M. Bernard
Fairfield University

H. Allan Dye
Purdue University

Rodney K. Goodyear
University of Southern California

Morag B. Colvin Harris
East Texas State University

Gordon M. Hart
Temple University

Elizabeth L. Holloway
University of Oregon

Everett L. Worthington
Virginia Commonwealth University

Geoffrey G. Yager
University of Cincinnati

A Publication of the
**Association for Counselor
Education and Supervision**
1987

A Division of the
American Counseling Association
5999 Stevenson Avenue
Alexandria, Virginia 22304

International Standard Book Number 1-55620-037-4

Foreword

Much attention has been given by the Association for Counselor Education and Supervision (ACES) to the curriculum of counselor education training programs, particularly with the recent emphasis on the accreditation process. During their preparation as counselors, students complete either a practicum or internship and, in most cases, both. For the faculty member, supervision of counseling practicums and internships/externships requires different skills and processes than the teaching of other courses in the curriculum.

Additionally, many graduates of our counselor education programs move into administrative positions as their careers advance. They may find themselves serving not only as counselors, but also as the director of a high school or college counseling center, director of a community mental health or rehabilitation center, or as a first line supervisor of other counselors within an educational or community setting. Very seldom, however, have counselors received training or course work related to the administrative and supervisory skills they are required to perform.

In order to address these needs, ACES initiated and has continued to support the Supervision Interest Network. A special focus was given when ACES selected "A Spectrum of Supervision" as its 1986-87 theme. The Network has undertaken several projects related to the supervision theme this year. These have included: preparing articles for ACES *Spectrum*, the Association newsletter, completing a summary report on a survey of syllabi for supervision courses, encouraging inclusion of standards for counseling supervisors in licensure laws, and addressing the need for didactic and experiential training in supervision skills as a part of the curriculum of approved programs and counseling sites.

In addition to these activities, a major contribution to the supervision theme has been the development of two handbooks. These two handbooks, entitled *Handbook of Counseling Supervision* and *Handbook of Administrative Supervision*, are intended to be practical guides which will provide resources for counselor educators to use with students in practicum and internship settings in their training programs, and for supervisors to use in the field for enhancing their own skills or for use with other counselors under their supervision. In addition, the handbooks can be used by instructors as textbooks or supplementary materials in supervision courses or workshops.

I am particularly proud to have had these two handbooks developed during my term of office, and I sincerely hope they are but the beginning of many efforts which will address the issue of counseling and administrative supervision in the coming years. Special mention and accolades should be given to Dr. L. DiAnne Borders and Dr. George Leddick, authors of the *Handbook of Counseling Supervision* and to Dr. Elizabeth Falvey, author of the *Handbook of Administrative Supervision*. These three individuals and others who contributed to the content or editing of the publications deserve special recognition. All of these ACES members have made an extraordinary contribution to their profession and the Association.

Nancy A. Scott, 1986-87 President
Association for Counselor Education and Supervision

Table of Contents

List of Figures

Introduction

Scenario one: You have just been assigned your first counseling student for counseling supervision. You volunteered for this experience with anticipation and enthusiasm, seeing it as an opportunity for your own professional development and as a way to contribute to the profession. As the first scheduled supervision session gets closer, however, you begin to wonder if you've taken on too much too soon. "What do I know about being a supervisor?" you ask yourself.

Scenario two: You have been supervising for several years and, although you were not trained specifically for this role, you have been relatively successful. Lately, however, you've noticed that supervision is not as exciting as it once was. You seem to be using the same approaches over and over. You are beginning to feel "stale."

Several studies have indicated that the typical supervisor has little preparation for the role (Hart & Falvey, 1986; Hess & Hess, 1983; Holloway, 1982; Loganbill & Hardy, 1983). If you are a doctoral student, you most likely have not had a supervision course and may not receive formal supervision of your first supervision experience (Allen, Szollos, & Williams, 1986; McColley & Baker, 1982). If you are a field supervisor, you most likely have a master's degree in counseling, and two or three years of counseling experience; you have not had a supervision theory course or in-service training in supervision (Hart & Falvey, 1986; Holloway, 1982). You rarely have an opportunity for in-service training in supervision strategies; if you are stuck or confused, you usually consult informally with a colleague (Hess & Hess, 1983). Even if you are an experienced counselor educator you probably have not been trained specifically in supervision (Hess & Hess, 1983).

The available evidence thus suggests that whether you are a novice or veteran, student or practitioner, you have probably had little preparation for the role of supervisor. This *Handbook* has been prepared for you. It has been designed to be an introduction to the procedures and process of counseling supervision, to the models, approaches, and interventions of supervision, and to the special concerns of the novice supervisor. It is

1

meant to be *practical*, covering the basics through defining a topic, summarizing relevant literature, and illustrating with sample forms and/or simulated problems. It is not bound to any particular theoretical approach to counseling or supervision but describes a "generic" process of supervision—the typical procedures you will follow, the interventions you will employ, and the problems you will encounter regardless of your counseling orientation. Its primary focus is individual supervision of individual counseling, although much of the content is relevant to supervision in a group setting of both individual and group counselors.

The *Handbook* will lead you through a sequential process of conducting supervision. We begin with a self-assessment of supervision-related skills, then proceed to an assessment of the supervisee, establishing goals and a contract, choosing interventions, dealing with process issues, considering legal and ethical concerns, and evaluating the supervisee. A last section helps you evaluate your own development and performance as a supervisor. Experienced supervisors may use selected sections to more clearly delineate their supervision style, identify areas they would like to develop, or learn a new intervention or approach to evaluation. Finally, an Epilogue summarizes literature on the beginning supervisor and describes instructional approaches for the instructor/supervisor of novice supervisors.

An underlying goal of the *Handbook* is to add substance to your identity as a supervisor, to facilitate "the important shift from thinking like a therapist to thinking like a supervisor" (Heath & Storm, 1983, p. 36). You are responsible for both a counselor and that counselor's clients, for the counselor's learning and the client's welfare. You will be a teacher, counselor, consultant, administrator, and evaluator. You will be challenged to translate your counseling methods into supervision interventions appropriate to your supervisee's needs, learning style, and ability level. You will be called on to be sensitive to the dynamics of both the counselor-client relationship and the supervisor-supervisee relationship.

One way to develop a mental image of yourself as a supervisor is to consider supervision as a matter of roles rather than of superiority at counseling. Although you may often have more counseling experience than your supervisees, this will not always be true. Yet, you can still be an effective supervisor regardless of the relative counseling competency of you and your supervisee. A supervisor is one who usually has a different perspective on counseling than the supervisee. While the supervisee can easily become embroiled in patterned interactions with the client, the supervisor can remain more objective because he or she does not have to respond directly to the client's interpersonal pulls. Some people become excellent supervisors because they are good observers, diagnosticians, and tactical and strategic planners. The important thing to remember is that as a supervisor you will be doing different things than you would as a counselor, and you need to begin to think of yourself as a supervisor even before your first session.

The *Handbook* covers the knowledge and skills basic to the identity of a supervisor. References are provided for further, in-depth reading on the topics. But, like other writers (Heath & Storm, 1983; Loganbill, Hardy, & Delworth, 1982), we encourage you to talk to other supervisors, since the process of becoming a "master supervisor" not only takes time but is immensely enriched through environmental support. As you prepare to meet your first or your hundreth supervisee, you have stepped into the role of a supervisor, and talking, thinking, and acting in that role will help you in creating and/or refining your own personal identity as a supervisor.

Chapter 1
Assessing Supervision Knowledge and Skills

Preparation for the role of supervisor can begin with a review of previous training and professional experiences relevant to the functions of a supervisor (Styczynski, 1980). A supervisor is called on to be a teacher, counselor, and consultant (Bernard, 1979; Boyd, 1978; Hart, 1982; Littrell, Lee-Borden, & Lorenz, 1979; Stenack & Dye, 1982; Stoltenberg, 1981), and most supervisors have had previous experience in one or more of these roles. Others may have served in another supervisory position (e.g., supervisor of student teacher or teaching assistant in pre-practicum), or have completed some coursework in counseling supervision. In addition, all supervisors have learned about supervision indirectly from experiences in the supervisee role.

From your experience as a counselor, you know how to establish a supportive working relationship with your supervisee, how to use your facilitative and challenging skills to promote growth; you are aware of the interpersonal dynamics in the supervisor-supervisee relationship. You also have knowledge of counseling theories and interventions to share with your supervisee.

If you have had teaching experience, you will be able to use your abilities to identify a supervisee's learning needs and preferred learning style. You can employ your skills in various instructional strategies to create an effective learning environment for your supervisee. You will also be familiar with the role of evaluator, both in devising appropriate methods of evaluation and in giving feedback.

Previous consulting experience will have given you an opportunity to assess a problem situation objectively and generate alternative solutions with the consultee assuming more control of the interaction. If you have previously been a supervisor, you have probably had experience in integrating some of the teaching, counseling, and consulting skills.

Research skills are also relevant for both gathering data and testing hypotheses about your supervisee (Styczynski, 1980). In addition, all supervisors have observed several role models while receiving counseling supervision. You probably have experienced a variety of supervision approaches and given feedback to peers (Styczynski, 1980). Through a self-assessment of these varied experiences in supervision-related roles, then, you can (a) identify relevant knowledge and skills already developed and (b) establish goals for areas needing development. This chapter outlines several procedures to conduct such a self-assessment.

Supervision Resumé

One way to facilitate the self-assessment of your supervision-related knowledge and skills is to construct a resumé of past experiences (Borders, 1983b). This resumé would list the experiences and describe the relevant skills and knowledge you developed from them.

To construct this resumé (Figure 1), first list the demographics of your work experience in the roles of teacher, counselor, consultant, and researcher. For example, for the teacher role, give your title (e.g., elementary teacher, instructor, inservice trainer), setting (e.g., high school, community college, agency), dates of employment, and the students you taught (e.g., gifted adolescents, returning adults in two-year liberal arts associate degree program). Also list special features of the setting (e.g., special program for pregnant teens). If you have been a supervisor in a work setting, include a description of this work also.

After you have described your experience in each role, identify the knowledge and skills you used in each role that are relevant to the functions of a supervisor. Figure 2 lists some related abilities to help you get started (based in part on Borders, 1983b; Stenack & Dye, 1982; Styczynski, 1980); add other skills you developed that will be useful to you as a supervisor. For each item, evaluate your competency using a scale of 1 (needs development) to 5 (expertise area), and then sum your ratings for each skill area.

The second major portion of the resumé (Figure 1) is a review of individual and group supervision of your own counseling. List your experiences as a supervisee (position, settings, dates, supervisor) and describe the supervision you received, including the techniques and styles of each supervisor. For example, did you review audiotapes and videotapes or report orally about your clients? How were these discussed? Did your supervisor have a particular emphasis? What was the supervisor's preferred counseling approach? What aspects of that approach were evident in your supervision sessions? How was your counseling evaluated?

Now describe and evaluate the abilities you have developed as a supervisee using Figure 3. Include any experiences as a peer supervisor during group supervision or other structured experiences (Borders, 1983b; Styczynski, 1980).

5

Qualitative self-assessment. Through constructing a resumé of your supervision-related experiences you have begun to develop a "profile" of your probable style, strengths, and limitations as a supervisor. The following questions are meant to further help you characterize your approach to supervision, specify your skills, and identify your learning goals:

1. In which supervision *role* (e.g., teacher, counselor, consultant) do you have the most experience? the least experience?
2. What was your preferred teaching style?
3. What was your preferred counseling style?
4. a. What consistent feedback have you received from your supervisors and students about your teaching (e.g., overexplained or verbose, balance of supportive and challenging evaluative feedback, able to give examples to illustrate concepts)?
   b. What consistent feedback have you received from your supervisors and clients about your counseling (e.g., constructive self-disclosure, able to deal with client resistance without being defensive, reluctant to confront)?
   c. How might these strengths and limitations be evidenced in your supervisory behavior?
5. With what types of learners (students) and clients were you most effective? least effective?
6. What counseling orientations and styles can you *effectively* and *comfortably* supervise?
7. Identify an *effective* and *ineffective* supervision intervention during your experiences as a supervisee. For each, describe what the supervisor said and did. Describe your reaction and response (thoughts, feelings, behavior) for each.
   a. What made the first incident an *effective* intervention? How did it fit your learning goals, learning style, and personal needs? Name a supervisee (or type of supervisee) for whom this could have been an *ineffective* intervention.
   b. What made the second incident an *ineffective* intervention? Name a supervisee (or type of supervisee) for whom this could have been an *effective* intervention.
   c. When might you use these interventions in your supervision?
8. Describe the type of supervision you preferred to receive and why you preferred it. Name a supervisee you know who had the same preferences. Name one who had different preferences. Describe both individuals' characteristics that may have influenced these different supervision preferences so you can recognize these characteristics in your supervisees.
9. What were your *expectations* of your supervisor and of supervision? How did your expectations change over time? Name a supervisee you know who had the same expectations. Name one who had different

expectations. Describe both individuals' characteristics that may have influenced these different supervision expectations so you can recognize these characteristics in your supervisees.

Based on your answers to these questions, describe your probable supervision style in 100 words, highlighting your areas of skill, knowledge, and strength. Then write five goals for what you hope to learn during supervision and ways you might reach these goals. For example, if you want to learn to use the "bug-in-the-ear" technique (Boylston & Tuma, 1972), you could read the relevant literature, observe a supervisor using the technique with a counselor, and ask another supervisor to use the technique with you during a counseling or supervision session.

Summary

In this section you have generated a resumé of your work experience, knowledge and skills as a supervisor. You have characterized your probable approach to supervision, identified your strengths, and written learning goals for areas needing improvement. You will now be able to describe your supervision style to your supervisees and ask other supervisors (your supervisor or peers) for feedback on specific areas. You will also be able to use more deliberately the knowledge and skills you have already developed.

Figure 1. Resumé format for a self-assessment of knowledge and skills developed in previous supervision-related roles and experiences.

Supervision-Related Skills and Knowledge

Name _____ Date _____

Teacher

   Date
                                                 Position, setting, students
                                                 Descriptive statement of
                                                 knowledge and skills

Counselor

   Date
                                                 Position, setting, clients
                                                 Descriptive statement of
                                                 knowledge and skills

Consultant

   Date
                                                 Position, setting, clients
                                                 Descriptive statement of
                                                 knowledge and skills

Researcher

   Date
                                                 Descriptive statement of
                                                 knowledge and skills

Supervisor

   Date
                                                 Position, setting,
                                                 supervisees
                                                 Descriptive statement of
                                                 knowledge and skills

Supervisee

   Date   Setting   Supervisor

    Mode of supervision

      Individual and/or Group
      Interventions (e.g., audiotapes, 'PR, casenotes)

    Supervisor's counseling orientation

  Supervisor's supervision style, including relationship/interpersonal

---

Figure 2. Self-assessment of supervision-related knowledge and skills.

Teaching Skills	Needs Development			Expertise	
Ability to identify learning needs of supervisee	1	2	3	4	5
Ability to identify learning style of supervisee	1	2	3	4	5
bility to write learning goals and objectives	1	2	3	4	5
Ability to devise instructional strategies to accommodate needs and learning style of supervisee	1	2	3	4	5
Ability to present material in a didactic manner	1	2	3	4	5
Ability to present material in an experiential manner (e.g., demonstrate, model)	1	2	3	4	5
Ability to explain the rationale for an intervention	1	2	3	4	5
Ability to evaluate supervisee's learning	1	2	3	4	5
Comfort in authority role	1	2	3	4	5
Ability to give constructive feedback to supervisee	1	2	3	4	5
Other _____	1	2	3	4	5
Counseling skills					
Ability to establish rapport, a working relationship with supervisee	1	2	3	4	5
Facilitative skills (e.g., warmth, primary empathy, genuineness, concreteness, etc.)	1	2	3	4	5
Challenging skills (e.g., self-disclosure, advanced empathy, confrontation, immediacy, etc.)	1	2	3	4	5
Ability to facilitate supervisee self-exploration of strengths, limitations, and concerns about counseling skills	1	2	3	4	5
Ability to help supervisee explore feelings about client, purposes of counseling, counseling interventions	1	2	3	4	5
Ability to help supervisee explore feelings about supervision	1	2	3	4	5
Ability to conduct intake sessions	1	2	3	4	5
Ability to conduct closure sessions	1	2	3	4	5
Ability to make referrals	1	2	3	4	5
Knowledge of interpersonal dynamics	1	2	3	4	5
Knowledge of counseling theories	1	2	3	4	5

Counseling skills cont.	Needs Development			Expertise	
Expertise in counseling techniques (specify)	1	2	3	4	5
Expertise with particular clients and issues (e.g., suicide, career)	1	2	3	4	5
Ability to identify themes, patterns of behavior	1	2	3	4	5
Ability to model counseling skills	1	2	3	4	5
Ability to respond with flexibility	1	2	3	4	5
Ability to integrate data about supervisee into comprehensive "case conceptualization"	1	2	3	4	5
Other _____	1	2	3	4	5

Consultation skills

	Needs Development			Expertise	
Ability to objectively assess problem situation	1	2	3	4	5
Ability to provide alternative interventions and/or conceptualizations of problem/client	1	2	3	4	5
Ability to facilitate supervisee brainstorming of alternatives, options, solutions	1	2	3	4	5
Ability to encourage supervisee to make own choices, take responsibility for decisions concerning client and counseling	1	2	3	4	5
Ability to function in more peer-like, collegial relationship with supervisee	1	2	3	4	5
Other _____	1	2	3	4	5

Research skills

	Needs Development			Expertise	
Ability to make accurate and reliable observations (of client and of supervisee)	1	2	3	4	5
Ability to state testable hypothesis (e.g., Is supervisee avoiding confrontation? Would role-playing be an effective supervision intervention?)	1	2	3	4	5
Ability to gather data relevant to testing hypothesis	1	2	3	4	5
Ability to evaluate hypothesis	1	2	3	4	5
Ability to incorporate new data, restate and retest hypothesis	1	2	3	4	5
Ability to identify confounding variables affecting change (e.g., supervisees' personal issues)	1	2	3	4	5
Ability to critically examine and incorporate new research into supervision (e.g., on counselor-client dynamics, assessment, counseling intervention, supervision intervention)	1	2	3	4	5
Other _____	1	2	3	4	5

Figure 3. Self-assessment of supervision-related abilities developed as a supervisee.

	Needs Development			Expertise	
Ability to evaluate audiotapes and videotapes	1	2	3	4	5
Ability to write case notes	1	2	3	4	5
Ability to identify strengths and areas for improvement	1	2	3	4	5
Ability to relate to supervisor	1	2	3	4	5
Ability to communicate needs to supervisor	1	2	3	4	5
Ability to plan and make case presentation	1	2	3	4	5
Ability to receive feedback	1	2	3	4	5
Willingness to be self-critical	1	2	3	4	5
Other _____	1	2	3	4	5

As peer supervisor

Ability to conceptualize case based on peer counselor's presentation	1	2	3	4	5
Ability to critique peer counselor's work	1	2	3	4	5
Ability to express suggestions and opinions with respect	1	2	3	4	5
Ability to receive feedback from peers	1	2	3	4	5
Ability to generalize indirect feelings from the supervision of peer counselors	1	2	3	4	5
Other _____	1	2	3	4	5

Chapter 2

Initial Supervisory Sessions: Working Contract and Assessment of the Supervisee

In your initial sessions with your supervisee there are several tasks you will need to accomplish:

1. Establish a working relationship,
2. Assess the supervisee's counseling skills,
3. Agree to a contract for the conduct of supervisory sessions, and
4. Establish learning goals for the supervisee.

If these tasks sound familiar, you are recognizing the similarities between supervision and counseling, teaching, or consulting. The English teacher, for example, asks students to write themes in order to evaluate their grammar, organization, and creative abilities. The counselor uses facilitative skills to join with a client and explore the client's issues, thus gathering verbal and nonverbal data about the client's level of functioning. Based on this information, the counselor writes a treatment plan of interventions and goals. The counselor and client also agree to a contract that may specify details ranging from the number of sessions to dealing with a client's suicidal tendencies.

During the first supervisory sessions, then, your task is to assess the supervisee's performance counseling skills, cognitive counseling skills, and his/her developmental level. Much like the assessment of a client or student, you will use these data to begin formulating a comprehensive "case conceptualization" of your supervisee, establish learning goals, and devise a "treatment plan" of appropriate supervision interventions. In addition, when a practicum or internship takes place in a field setting, you need to request a meeting of all the persons involved (i.e., university supervisor, field supervisor, supervisee) to negotiate a contract that specifies requirements, expectations, goals, evaluation procedures, and contact between the supervisors.

First Meeting—Relationship and Contract

The first meeting with your supervisee should be scheduled before he/she sees clients so you can have time to get acquainted. Heath and Storm (1983) believe it is important to demonstrate respect for your supervisee during this first meeting, and suggest you ask the supervisee to describe previous experiences in supervision, preferred counseling approaches, and preferred supervision approaches. You can describe your supervision style based on your previous self-assessment (Chapter 1). This exchange will provide the basis for negotiating a way to work together during supervision (Heath & Storm, 1983). It is particularly important to be sensitive to your supervisee's negative supervision experiences (if any) that may be influencing him/her to be cautious or resistant to supervisory feedback.

By the end of the first meeting, you and your supervisee will need to have clear expectations about supervision. A verbal or written contract might include the following:

1. How frequently will you meet, for how long, and where?

2. How will you use audiotapes, videotapes, case notes, etc., in supervision? For example, will you review one videotape in supervision together and take two audiotapes to review yourself between sessions? Will the tapes reviewed in-session be the same or different clients each week? How should the supervisee prepare a tape for in-session supervision (e.g., pre-select segments; complete a standard evaluation form for each session)? How will confidentiality of the client be assured?

3. What structure or procedure will you follow each supervision session? For example, will you begin with a brief review of each client, an audiotape, or the supervisee's specific requests/questions?

4. How will you handle "emergency" situations (e.g., suicidal clients)? How can your supervisee reach you? What does the supervisee do if you are unavailable?

5. How will the supervisee be evaluated? What criteria will be used? Will you be responsible for assigning a grade for practicum or internship? Write a narrative evaluation of strengths and areas for improvement? Complete a standard evaluation form provided by the university counselor education program or agency? Will there be a formal midterm evaluation of the supervisee?

6. With what type of clients will the supervisee work? Who does the screening and assignment of clients? Can the supervisee express preferences (e.g., career clients, adolescents, couples)? What happens if there is an insufficient number of clients to provide the supervisee with enough experience to fulfill practicum or internship requirements?

7. If you are a university-based supervisor, will you be visiting the supervisee's field site? How often? What will you do on these visits (e.g., meet with the field supervisor, observe the supervisee)? How will the supervisee need to prepare for your visit?

The relevance and importance of these issues will, of course, vary according to the setting (e.g., university in-house practicum lab, community mental health agency, public school), clients served (e.g., recovering drug addicts, students, families), and predetermined requirements or restrictions. It is important, then, to investigate the parameters of the setting, the expectations of the university counselor education program, relevant legal considerations, and any other factors specific to the supervisee's situation and to your role and responsibilities as a supervisor before the first meeting. You will be able to provide pertinent information to your supervisee, develop an appropriate and accurate contract, and establish a reassuring, informed relationship.

Assessment of Supervisee

Before the first supervision meeting you also want to consider how you will assess the supervisee's counseling skills. The initial assessment will probably span several supervisory sessions, will include both your evaluation and the supervisee's self-evaluation, and will serve as the basis for a joint statement of learning goals for supervision.

A supervisee's self-assessment of counseling skills, much like your self-evaluation (Chapter 1), is a valuable source of information. The supervisee's own statement gives you an indication of the skill deficiencies and areas of concern on which the supervisee wants to focus, and the competencies and experiences upon which he/she can build. In addition, paying attention to this self-statement is another way to communicate respect to your supervisee.

The format of the initial assessment conducted by you and your supervisee may be informal and/or formal, verbal and/or written, although the more concrete it is the easier it will be to translate the assessment statements into goal statements, monitor progress, and evaluate changes. This section presents a variety of procedures you and your supervisee may use to assess his/her performance skills, cognitive counseling skills, and developmental level.

Counseling performance skills. Counseling performance skills refer to what the counselor does during a session or his/her counseling behaviors. Included are the basic helping or facilitative skills (e.g., warmth, genuineness, concreteness, primary and advanced empathy, self-disclosure, confrontation, and immediacy), theoretically-based techniques (e.g., two-chair exercise, systematic desensitization, reframing), more procedural skills (e.g., opening and closing a session), and those that are issue specific (e.g., assessing lethality of suicidal clients).

To assess counseling performance skills you might ask the supervisee to tape an initial session to review together during your next meeting or for you to review beforehand. If you are a field supervisor, you might choose to meet with the counselor just prior to and following the first counseling session, then observe or even sit in on that first session. A role-play of a counseling session with the supervisee also provides an opportunity to observe verbal and nonverbal behavior, and may be especially appropriate for the novice counselor (Weiner & Kaplan, 1980).

Choice of a more formal assessment tool will depend on the experience level of the supervisee, the skills emphasized by your orientation, and whether your supervisee will also use the assessment tool. Many university counseling programs have devised rating scales of basic skills for evaluating pre-practicum and practicum interviews that you may adapt for your assessment of the supervisee. One example is E. Gordon Poling's rating form (Figure 4).

The Barrett-Lennard Relationship Inventory (BLRI; Barrett-Lennard, 1962), is a standardized measure of facilitative conditions (e.g., empathy, regard, congruence, unconditionality of regard). Rating scales for specific facilitative skills include those by Gazda et al. (1984). In contrast, the Vanderbilt Psychotherapy Process Scales (VPPS; O'Malley, Suh, & Strupp, 1983; Strupp, 1981) can be used to rate more advanced counseling skills, such as identifying themes and patterns in client behavior, reframing the client's perspective of self or a situation, and helping clients assess the consequences of and take responsibility for their actions. Two other scales, the Hill Counselor Verbal Response Category System (Hill, 1978) and the Inventory of Counselor Behaviors (ICB; Dustin, Engen, & Shymansky, 1982), describe counselor verbal responses using categories such as approval/praise, open or closed questions, reflection, explanation, and confrontation. These same scales can also be used in the final evaluation to measure growth.

Holahan and Galasssi (1986), for example, used a systematic approach combining initial assessment and final evaluation of a supervisee's listening skills. An informal assessment based on simple frequency counts of questions, paraphrases, and reflections of feelings in early counseling sessions indicated frequent use of closed-ended questions and few reflective statements. The researchers then conducted a more systematic analysis of randomly selected segments of counseling interviews using Hill's criteria (Hill, 1978). These baseline data served as a basis for comparison with analysis of interviews during and after supervision.

A comprehensive assessment procedure is Ponterotto and Zander's (1984) multimodal approach to supervision. Their approach includes assessment of the supervisee's Behavior, Affect, Sensations, Images, Cognitions, Interpersonal functioning, Diet and Drugs (BASIC-ID; Lazarus, 1981). The supervisor and supervisee compile their separate assessments into one Modality Profile that details the antecedents of difficulty areas. For example, a supervisee thinks negative self-statements ("What if I can't think of an appropriate response?"), then worries, gets tight muscles, and doesn't think

15

of responses spontaneously in the counseling session. Like all assessment tools, the Modality Profile can become the basis for choosing supervision interventions.

Cognitive counseling skills. Cognitive counseling skills refer to how the counselor thinks about the client and chooses interventions. These conceptualization skills are difficult for beginning counselors to develop (Fuqua, Johnson, Anderson, & Newman, 1984), and have received less attention from counselor educators and supervisors than overt behavioral counseling skills (Bernier, 1980; Claiborn & Dixon, 1982; Loganbill & Stoltenberg, 1983). In contrast to models for teaching facilitative skills and counseling techniques, there are few established approaches for teaching a supervisee how to sort through and integrate client information and to form effective clinical hypotheses (Holloway & Wolleat, 1980). Beginning supervisees may even need help in identifying what client data they are attending to and how they process that information before they can learn what data are relevant and how to utilize them effectively. Assessing cognitive counseling skills may be especially appropriate with more advanced supervisees who are ready to develop more sophisticated case conceptualizations and clinical hypotheses.

The contents of supervisees' initial case notes are one indication of the level of their case conceptualization skills (Presser & Pfost, 1985). Notice whether they focus only on the client, or if they include observations of their own behavior and counselor-client interactions.

For an informal assessment of a supervisee's in-session processing, a supervisor may ask the supervisee a series of questions about specific interventions while reviewing a tape of an early session (Bernstein, Hofmann, & Wade, 1986; Bernstein & Lecomte, 1979):
1. What was I hearing my client say and/or seeing my client do?
2. What was I thinking about my observations?
3. What were my alternatives to say or do at this point?
4. How did I choose from among the alternatives?
5. How did I intend to proceed with my selected response(s)?

The supervisee's answers to these questions would indicate the conceptualization and decision-making processes used during counseling.

You may also use an adaptation of Interpersonal Process Recall (IPR; Kagan, 1980) to assess a counselor's cognitive processes and skills. To use IPR, a supervisor reviews a videotape of a counseling session with a counselor, asking the counselor to describe underlying thoughts, feelings, and intentions during the session. The supervisor, functioning as an "inquirer," facilitates the recall of thoughts and feelings and discourages critical self-evaluation. By using IPR with an early counseling session, a supervisor may glean clues regarding what client data the supervisee does and does not attend to and how those data are employed in making decisions about interventions.

Standardized assessments of a supervisee's cognitive processes and/or case conceptualization skills include the Intentions List (Hill & O'Grady, 1985), the Clinical Assessment Questionnaire (Holloway & Wolleat, 1980), and the Written Treatment Planning Simulation (Butcher, Scofield, & Baker, 1985). The supervisee might also complete a case conceptualization format (e.g., Hulse & Jennings, 1984; Loganbill & Stoltenberg, 1983) with an initial client (see Chapter 4 for descriptions of these instruments).

Developmental level. Developmental models of counseling supervision (e.g., Gaoni & Neumann, 1974; Grater, 1985; Hart, 1982; Hogan, 1964; Littrell, Lee-Borden, & Lorenz, 1979; Loganbill, Hardy, & Delworth, 1982; Stoltenberg, 1981) describe a "generic" process of counselor growth regardless of counselor theoretical orientation. These models describe counselor growth as a series of sequential, hierarchal stages. Supervisees gradually develop a personal and professional identity as a counselor, a growth process that is continuous and ongoing across the professional lifespan.

In early stages supervisees are dependent and imitative, use categorical thinking, and lack awareness of their motivations and skills. As they begin to define themselves as counselors, they experience both internal conflict, feeling confusion, assurance, and doubt, and external conflict in their efforts to be more independent of the supervisor. Then, as they improve their skills and gain experience and confidence, they become more flexible, tolerant, and insightful, and move to a more peer-like collegial relationship with the supervisor. The results of related research studies tend to support a developmental perspective of supervision (e.g., Cross & Brown, 1983; Friedlander & Ward, 1984; Heppner & Roehlke, 1984; Hill, Charles, & Reed, 1981; McNeill, Stoltenberg, & Pierce, 1985; Miars et al., 1983; Moskowitz, 1981; Nash, 1975; Nelson, 1978; Rabinowitz, Heppner, & Roehlke, 1986; Reising & Daniels, 1983; Wiley & Ray, 1986; Worthington, 1984; Worthington & Roehlke, 1979; Worthington & Stern, 1985; Zucker & Worthington, 1986).

Hill et al. (1981), for example, studied counseling psychology students throughout their doctoral training. They found that the students went through four stages roughly paralleling Stoltenberg's (1981) theoretical model of counselor development. The first stage was characterized by counselor anxiety and self-focus. The second stage involved counselors adopting a "counselor stance," in which they adhered to some theory of counseling they had read about or been taught by a professor or supervisor. Failures in counseling were attributed to the counselor's inability to perform theoretically-prescribed techniques. As counselors gained experience, attributions changed and the counselors began to challenge theoretical precepts until they reached a stage of confusion. Ultimately, counselors developed integrated personal styles that fit their personality and clientele.

Assessment of developmental level, then, can help identify professional and personal issues a supervisee is facing and suggest appropriate supervision interventions. As the descriptions of the stages indicate, amount of experience is a first step in assessing a supervisee's developmental level. Stoltenberg (1981) and Loganbill et al. (1982), however, emphasize that supervisees' individual attributes, such as needs, motivations, and cognitive-developmental level, will influence the rate of growth through the developmental stages. Research has indicated that experience level and developmental level are not equivalent (e.g., Borders, Fong, & Neimeyer, 1986; Stoltenberg, Solomon, & Ogden, 1986; Wiley & Ray, 1986).

There are tools for assessing the stages or levels described in two developmental models. Stoltenberg (1981), for example, describes cognitive and personality characteristics of supervisees at four levels of development (i.e., dependency, dependency-autonomy conflict, conditional dependence, and master counselor). Recently, Wiley and Ray (1986) elaborated the "counselor complexity model" to create the Supervision Level Scale (SLS), a measure of (a) degree of confidence in present counseling skills, (b) insight about one's impact on clients, (c) preference for a theoretical framework, (d) sense of professional identity, and (e) awareness of limitations in counseling for supervisees at each developmental level. The Supervisee Levels Questionnaire (McNeill, Stoltenberg, & Pierce, 1985), also based on Stoltenberg's (1981) model, measures supervisees' perceptions of their level of development in self-awareness, dependency—autonomy, and theory/skills acquisition. Both instruments are relatively new and require further testing to determine reliability and validity.

In addition, Hardy and Loganbill have devised an assessment chart (Figure 5) to determine supervisee developmental level as defined in their model (Loganbill et al., 1982). They present a three-stage model of supervision that presumes a supervisee will be functioning at different stages for eight supervisory issues (i.e., competence, emotional awareness, autonomy, identity, respect for individual differences, purpose and direction, personal motivation, professional ethics). Rather than a strictly hierarchal model, they propose a more cyclical process as supervisees experience each supervisory issue in the three stages of (a) stagnation (a period of latency, naive unawareness, "stuckness," avoidance, and black-and-white thinking),(b) confusion (a period of instability, conflict, and feelings of incompetence resulting from the awareness of one's limitations), and (c) integration (a period of stability and flexibility, with an understanding of one's strengths and weaknesses and a sense of continued growth).

Loganbill et al. (1982) do not suggest a typical sequence in confronting the eight issues, but believe each supervisee follows a unique pattern of growth. The supervisor, then, assesses a supervisee's behaviors and attitudes for each issue to determine the level of functioning (stage) for each separate issue.

Summary

Your comprehensive assessment of the supervisee is somewhat analogous to the case conceptualization of a client, except that you are focusing on the supervisee's *professional* issues. Loganbill and Stoltenberg's (1983) case conceptualization format can be adapted to summarize your assessment:

1. Relevant demographic data (e.g., age, sex, race, marital status).
2. "Presenting problem" or supervisee's learning goals and needs.
3. Relevant history (e.g., academic coursework, previous counseling and supervision experience, level of competency of performance and cognitive counseling skills).
4. Interpersonal style (e.g., general attitude toward clients and supervisor, view of the counselor-client relationship).
5. Environmental factors (e.g., the counseling setting; stressors and supports in supervisee's life).
6. Personality dynamics
    (a) Cognitive factors (e.g., positive and negative cognitions about self as counselor; level of insight into own and client's dynamics; case conceptualization skills; ability to generate hypotheses and make decisions about interventions).
    (b) Emotional factors (e.g., ability to respond to variety of emotions of clients).
7. Summary conceptualization of supervisee, integrating the above.

In your first few supervision sessions you have established a working relationship with your supervisee, and clarified expectations and procedures (you and your supervisee agree how supervision will be conducted). You have assessed the supervisee's performance and cognitive counseling skills and developmental level, and so are ready to determine learning goals and then choose appropriate supervision interventions for reaching these goals.

Figure 4. Counseling practicum interview rating form.

_____ Audiotape   Interview Date _____

_____ Videotape   Counselor _____

_____ Other (Specify)   Supervisor/Rater _____

Specific Criteria	Rating (best to least)	Remarks
1. OPENING: Was opening unstructured, friendly, and pleasant? Any role definition needed? Any introduction necessary?	5 4 3 2 1	
2. RAPPORT: Did counselor establish good rapport with counselee? Was the stage set for a productive interview?	5 4 3 2 1	
3. INTERVIEW RESPONSIBILITY: If not assumed by counselee, did counselor assume appropriate level of responsibility for interview conduct? Counselor or counselee initiative?	5 4 3 2 1	
4. INTERACTION: Were the counselee and counselor really communicating in a meaningful manner?	5 4 3 2 1	
5. ACCEPTANCE/PERMISSIVENESS: Was the counselor accepting and permissive of counselee emotions, feelings, and expressed thoughts?	5 4 3 2 1	
6. REFLECTION OF FEELINGS: Did counselor reflect and react to feelings or did interview remain on an intellectual level?	5 4 3 2 1	
7. COUNSELOR RESPONSES: Were counselor responses appropriate in view of what the counselee was expressing or were responses concerned with trivia and minutia? Meaningful questions?	5 4 3 2 1	
8. VALUE MANAGEMENT: How did the counselor cope with values? Were attempts made to impose counselor values during the interview?	5 4 3 2 1	
9. COUNSELING RELATIONSHIP: Was counselor-counselee relationship conducive to productive counseling? Was a counseling relationship established?	5 4 3 2 1	

Specific Criteria	Rating (best to least)	Remarks
10. CLOSING: Was closing counselor or counselee initiated? Was it abrupt or brusque? Any follow-up or further interview scheduling accomplished?	5 4 3 2 1	
11. GENERAL TECHNIQUES: How well did the counselor conduct the mechanics of the interview?	5 4 3 2 1	

A. Duration of interview: Was the interview too long or too short? Should interview have been terminated earlier or later?

B. Vocabulary level: Was counselor vocabulary appropriate for the counselee?

C. Mannerisms: Did the counselor display any mannerisms which might have adversely affected the interview or portions thereof?

D. Verbosity: Did the counselor dominate the interview, interrupt, override, or become too wordy?

E. Silences: Were silences broken to meet counselor needs or were they dealt with in an effective manner?

COMMENTS FOR COUNSELOR ASSISTANCE: Additional comments that might assist the counselor in areas not covered by the preceding suggestions.

This form was developed by E. Gordon Poling, Chair, Division of Educational Psychology and Counseling, University of South Dakota, Vermillon, SD. A similar version was published in Dimick, K. M., & Krause, F. H. (1980). Practicum manual for counseling and psychotherapy *(pp. 279-280). Muncie, IN: Accelerated Development. Reprinted by permission of Dr. Poling and Accelerated Development.*

Figure 5. Assessment of supervisee developmental level.

CRITICAL ISSUES IN SUPERVISION	Stage 1 Stagnation Stability	Stage 2 Confusion	Stage 3 Integration
1. *Issues of Competence.* Skills. Technique. Mastery. Ability to take appropriate action.			
2. *Issues of Emotional Awareness.* Knowing oneself. Differentiation of feelings. Ability to use own reactions/emotions diagnostically.			
3. *Issues of Autonomy.* Sense of one's own choices/decisions. Independence and self-directedness to appropriate degree. Sense of self.			
4. *Issues of Identity.* Theoretical consistency. Conceptual integration. Sense of self as therapist/counselor.			
5. *Issues of Respect for Individual Differences.* Deep and basic respect. Active effort to understand. Appreciation of differences.			
6. *Issues of Purpose and Direction.* Formulation of treatment plan and appropriate long- and short-term goals. Cognitive map of progress.			
7. *Issues of Personal Motivation.* Personal drives and meaning. Reward satisfaction. Complex and evolving nature of motivation.			
8. *Issues of Professional Ethics.* Legal issues. Values. Professional standards. Integration of these into ongoing practice.			

Adapted from Chickering's 7 vectors of development. Chickering, A.W. (1969). Education and identity. San Francisco: Jossey-Bass.

This chart was taken from Hardy, E., & Loganbill, C. (1986, August). Clinical supervision workshop. Continuing education workshop at the annual meeting of the American Psychological Association, Washington, DC. Reprinted by permission of Dr. Hardy and Dr. Loganbill.

Chapter 3

Goals for Supervision

Establishing learning goals with your supervisee can facilitate your work together in several ways. Active involvement of the supervisee is crucial; a statement of goals you have mutually agreed upon enhances supervisee commitment to the goals and fosters a cooperative relationship. If goals are small and presented in specific steps, supervisees can experience success critical to future motivation. In teaching supervisees to set goals for their own development, you are also modeling the process they may employ with clients. Finally, goal identification is successful because it provides structure for the learning program in supervision and clarifies expectations in supervision.

Writing Goal Statements

Draw upon your teaching experience in writing learning objectives and/or your counseling experience in establishing client goals as you help your supervisee create an initial goal statement. Novice counselors often need to be taught basic principles for setting attainable goals (Martin, Hiebert, & Marx, 1981). Supervisees are most likely to achieve counseling competencies if they identify (a) a specific, observable goal, (b) the action steps necessary to reach the goal, and (c) ways to recognize evidence that they've reached the goal (Mager, 1961). The following example, an excerpt from an exercise written by Harold Hackney (1976) for supervisees in first practicum, illustrates the three components of effective goal setting:

1. *Goal:* Focus on affect. Respond to affective content of client statements.

2. *Action Step:* Each time I hear an emotion word in the client's statement, I will respond with a statement that reflects that feeling.

3. *Evidence:* Upon analysis of audio (or video) tape, I will have responded to 80 percent of the emotion words stated by the client.

23

While both long-term and short-term goals are important, supervisees may especially need help identifying short-term goals leading to a long-term goal, and the sequential action steps toward the short-term goal. The following is an example of clarifying a manageable action plan toward a long-term goal:

Long-term goal: Be able to use several Gestalt techniques (performance skill). Identify when and with what clients the approaches are most effective (cognitive skill).

Short-term goal: Use a two-chair exercise with an appropriate client.

Steps in action plan: (a) Read about two-chair exercise in several sources; watch film of counselor using exercise; (b) With supervisor, identify client and issue for two-chair exercise; discuss together the rationale for the choice of this client; (c) Write out dialogue for introducing and explaining exercise to client; (d) Role play with peer and/or supervisor; (e) Improve plan based on feedback; (f) Use exercise with client; (g) Review videotape of session with supervisor and evaluate performance.

Evidence of progress toward goals for some skills, such as those involved in case conceptualization, are not directly observable during a counseling session. Giving specific feedback during supervision is necessary to help the supervisee measure improvement in these skill areas.

Supervisor's Goals vs. Supervisee's Goals

Your assessments have probably provided information about supervisee learning needs, especially cognitive counseling skills and developmental issues, that are beyond the conscious awareness of the supervisee. Most novice counselors, for example, want to learn new techniques but seldom verbalize a cognitive skill goal concerning the rationale for the choice of an intervention with a particular client or issue. A novice's more inexperienced and simplistic view is to learn *the* technique to use with a particular type of client or particular issue. As a supervisor, then, you may have an additional goal of helping the novice counselor begin to realize that a particular technique is not always *the* correct intervention in similar situations. You may find more advanced supervisees need help in conceptualizing clients from more than one theoretical perspective. In short, it may be necessary for you to verbalize goals for developing cognitive counseling skills with most supervisees.

You have also identified developmental issues in your assessment of the supervisee, and these additional dynamics will influence your supervision goals and choice of interventions. An appropriate long-term goal for a novice counselor, for example, is to encourage independence, gradually becoming less instructive and answering fewer questions about specific interventions (Stoltenberg, 1981), or to bring into awareness how the novice's naive and stereotypic attitudes affect interactions with clients of other cultures and ethnic groups (Loganbill et al., 1982). In contrast, you can help the more advanced supervisee begin to form an integrated, theoretically-consistent professional identity. The results of your developmental assessment, then, may indicate additional, perhaps unspoken, goals, and influence how you intervene to help supervisees move toward their specified goals.

Setting Realistic Goals

As a result of the assessments you and your supervisee completed, you have a wealth of information to use in writing learning goals for supervision. It is important at this point to avoid overwhelming both your supervisee and yourself with how much can, should, or needs to be learned (Styczynski, 1980). Similar to your work with students and clients, you want to set realistic goals that will help develop the supervisee's confidence and competence.

Your assessment of the supervisee's performance and cognitive skill levels and developmental issues can help you prioritize and sequence goals based on the supervisee's needs and level of readiness. Improving confrontation skills, for example, may first require teaching the supervisee basic assertiveness skills or how to identify discrepancies between client verbal and nonverbal communication. Similarly, a highly anxious novice counselor cannot objectively evaluate the impact of an intervention until he/she gains confidence and is able to focus more on the client's reactions and responses.

Loganbill et al.'s (1982) developmental model also emphasizes the prioritizing of goals. After assessing the supervisee's level of functioning (stage) for each of the eight developmental issues, the supervisor determines which issues need to be moved from stage one to stage two or from stage two to stage three, and which issues need to be left at the current stage. Use of the authors' assessment chart (Figure 5) can help you recognize how many issues are already in the second stage of Confusion and avoid overwhelming your supervisee (and yourself) by trying to work on too many issues at once. Which issues can be left at the first Stagnation or Stability stage for the time being? Which issues are at the third Integration stage and can provide a base of confidence and strength to support supervisees while they struggle with stage two Confusion issues?

It is also important to recognize that goals can and will be rewritten as goals are met, as you learn more about your supervisee, and as the supervisee gains self-awareness and confidence. Assessment, goal-setting, and evaluation are continuous and overlapping processes throughout supervision.

Monitoring Progress toward Goals

Just as with goal setting, it is important to build in opportunities for supervisees to evaluate their progress toward their goals, so that they can experience success and gain confidence in their abilities. If goal statements meet the criteria previously described (i.e., specific, observable goal, action steps, evidence), supervisees will be able to evaluate their actions and subsequently write new goals.

25

One approach supervisees may use to monitor progress toward their individualized goals is the portfolio method (Atkinson & Zimmer, 1977) adapted from the procedure art students use to demonstrate their abilities and illustrate their best work. Supervisees compile a folder that demonstrates competencies, including self-assessments, audiotapes of counseling sessions with corresponding self and supervisor feedback, case studies, session notes demonstrating case conceptualization, and written reports of clients. In another application of the portfolio method, supervisees keep an "individualized learning program" file that includes the goal statements, action plans, and evaluations generated over the semester. By using the portfolio method to evidence goal attainment, supervisees become more responsible for their own growth, and they can transfer the folder from one supervisor to the next.

Forsyth and Ivey (1980) suggest counselors can use microcounseling procedures to monitor changes in skills. A typescript of a session is scored using the microcounseling taxonomy, counting the number of times a specific type of response was used. A supervisee, for example, can evaluate whether he/she is using fewer close-ended questions and more reflective statements.

Self-supervision (Bernstein, Hofmann, & Wade, 1986; Bernstein & Lecomte, 1979) is another approach that may be taught to supervisees for evaluating their performance toward goals in each session. Incorporating both performance and cognitive counseling skills, the self-supervision model also promotes professional autonomy, one goal of developmental models of supervision. The model outlines a series of sequential steps and questions supervisees ask themselves as they recycle through this procedure (see Bernstein et al., 1986, for examples):

1. *Self-observation* (linking counselor thoughts, feelings, and actions with client behaviors):
   a) What was I hearing my client say and/or seeing my client do?
   b) What was I thinking about my observations?
   c) What were my alternatives to say or to do at this point?
   d) How did I choose from among the alternatives?
   e) How did I intend to proceed with my selected response(s)?
   f) What did I actually say or do?
2. *Self-assessment* (evaluating counselor performance by observing client response):
   a) What effects did my response have on my client?
   b) How, then, would I evaluate the effectiveness of my response?
3. Selecting a goal (targeting behaviors or cognitions to change).
4. Planning for change (using written resources and/or a consultant).
5. Implementation of plan.
6. Readjustment of plan based on increasing self-knowledge.

As a supervisor you will also be monitoring your supervisee's progress. These may take the form of "case notes" for each supervision session, summarizing (a) issues the supervisee presented, (b) results of the supervisee's attempts to put goals into action (e.g., your evaluation based on tapes or live observation of counseling session), (c) your interventions, (d) your assessment of progress, and (e) your plans for the next session. You may also want to periodically use your assessment tool(s) (e.g., rating scale of audiotaped counseling session) and compare the results with your assessment data.

Professional Development "Assignments"

You may make additional assignments to foster the supervisee's development of an identity as a counselor. These assignments, designed to reflect the actual work of a professional, might include the following:

1. Attend one counseling-related conference or workshop; write or present a summary and critique.

2. Create a file of referrals you use or could use as a counselor (e.g., crisis and suicide services, shelters for abused spouses and children, drug abuse treatment centers, Alcoholics Anonymous). List the name of the group or agency, address, phone number, contact person, and a short description of the services.

3. Visit one referral agency and interview the contact person about the services.

Supervisees might also create an annotated bibliography for a recurring supervision issue (e.g., dealing with angry clients) or an unfamiliar client issue (e.g., grief). These assignments encourage professional involvement in the community and foster an expectation for continual professional development.

Summary

At this point your supervisee has an initial statement of specific, observable, and measurable goals, a listing of action steps towards these goals, and methods of evaluating progress. Even so, the supervisee will need your help in taking the action steps, evaluating performance, and identifying stumbling blocks to professional growth. In addition, based on your more comprehensive assessment, you have additional goals in terms of the supervisee's developmental needs.

If you view assessment of the supervisee as analogous to case conceptualization, then supervision goals can be described as the first step in a "treatment plan" for supervision. In the next chapter you will begin to select "treatment modalities" or supervision interventions to help your supervisee meet the goals each of you has written.

Chapter 4

Choosing and Implementing Supervision Interventions

You are now ready to select the supervision interventions that will best help your particular supervisee make progress toward reaching the goals the two of you have written. This chapter will discuss considerations for choosing interventions and briefly describe some representative supervision approaches. These approaches focus on the supervisee's development and do not include those instances when you choose direct intervention to protect the welfare of the client.

Choosing Interventions

Your choice of interventions will be based on several factors, including the following:
1. The supervisee's own learning goals.
2. The supervisee's experience level and developmental issues.
3. The supervisee's learning style.
4. Your goals for the supervisee.
5. Your theoretical orientation.
6. Your own learning goals for this supervisory experience.

A wide variety of interventions is described in the literature. Most are appropriate for supervisees at each level of development, depending on how you apply the intervention (Borders, 1986); most may also be adapted for working on performance or cognitive counseling skills. A microtraining approach, for example, can be used to teach a basic facilitative skill (e.g., minimal encourager) or a more advanced skill (e.g., direct-mutual communication) (Forsyth & Ivey, 1980). Similarly, an IPR procedure can help an anxious, self-focused novice counselor to attend to client nonverbal behavior, stimulate an intern's awareness of transference and countertransference, and help all supervisees clarify intentions and rationale for counseling interventions. Therefore, you need to consider not only what interventions you want to use, but also how they can best be employed with your particular supervisee (Borders, 1986).

Developmental level of supervisee. Developmental models (e.g., Gaoni & Neumann, 1974; Grater, 1985; Hart, 1982; Hogan, 1964; Littrell et al., 1979; Loganbill et al., 1982; Stoltenberg, 1981) provide one framework for selecting and implementing interventions; they also indicate what role (e.g., teacher, counselor, consultant) will be predominant at each developmental level. Beginning counselors, for example, tend to depend on the supervisor for instructions and support. They focus on counseling performance skills, are highly task-oriented, and want to know what, when, where, why, and how counseling is to be accomplished. They prefer direct teaching approaches such as didactic presentations, observation of the supervisor counseling a client, reading assignments, suggestions for appropriate counseling interventions, discussions linking theory and practice, modeling, and role-playing. They also want this structure within a supportive and encouraging environment (Moskowitz, 1981; Nash, 1975; Rabinowitz et al., 1986; Worthington & Roehlke, 1979).

As supervisees gain experience, confidence, and competence, they prefer less directive supervision and begin to view the supervisor as a resource person who shares ideas and learns along with the supervisee. Ready to focus more on cognitive counseling skills, they prefer discussions of theoretical issues and case conceptualizations. In addition, they want their supervisors to be more confrontive about personal issues (e.g., transference and countertransference) affecting therapy (Heppner & Roehlke, 1984; McNeill et al., 1985; Reising & Daniels, 1983).

As more advanced supervisees develop their own professional style and integrated identity as counselors, they function more independently and report a peer-like, consultative relationship with supervisors (Hill et al., 1981). More aware of their strengths and limitations, they take more responsibility for the focus of supervision. Interventions and topics for supervision are chosen through cooperative discussion and mutual agreement between the supervisor and counselor.

Your assessment of your supervisee's developmental level, then, can help you identify both the type of interventions and the kind of relationship that will best promote learning and development. Developmental models emphasize the responsibility of the supervisor to take a proactive role in facilitating supervisee growth (Borders, 1986). Stoltenberg (1981), for example, describes the effective supervisor as one who recognizes the strengths, needs, and learning style of each supervisee and creates the appropriate learning environment. (Descriptions of these "optional supervision environments" have been elaborated in Wiley & Ray, 1986.) In Loganbill et al.'s (1982) model, the supervisor determines which of the eight developmental issues need to be moved from stage one to two or from stage two to three, and which issues need to be left at the current stage.

Based on this prioritizing of needs, supervisors choose from facilitative, confrontive, conceptual, prescriptive, and catalytic interventions to facilitate development.

Blocher (1983) describes a "developmental learning environment" that is characterized by challenge, involvement, support, structure, feedback, innovation, and integration. The supervisor provides a balance of challenge and support, of innovation and integration, in that environment. Developmental models suggest that balance will vary based on the experience level and individual attributes of a supervisee.

Learning style of supervisee. Supervisees also differ in their preferred approach to learning (Stoltenberg, 1981). Ivey and Authier (1978) have observed, for example, that counseling students respond differently to the parts of the microtraining paradigm. They find students vary in their preference for self-observation, videotape models, written manuals, and the assistance of a supportive supervisor.

Some supervisees learn best by understanding the theoretical framework of a new skill first, while others prefer to begin with observation or more experiential learning-by-doing. Supervision interventions that initially compliment the supervisee's learning style can enhance their involvement and their development. In reinforcing learning, additional teaching approaches can give the practical-oriented student necessary theoretical background and help the conceptual learner translate concepts into action. Supervisees' preferences for feedback mode and rewards will also vary by individual motivation style (Stoltenberg, 1981). Some will respond best to the supervisor's warmth, praise, and support, for example, while others will prefer a more objective critique of counseling performance.

Theoretical orientation. The content of supervision has historically been tied to a counseling theory (Bartlett, 1983; Holloway & Hosford, 1983; Leddick & Bernard, 1980). Supervision approaches and techniques, for example, have evolved from the therapeutic approaches described in psychoanalytic (Eckstein & Wallerstein, 1972; Moldawsky, 1980; Mueller & Kell, 1972), client-centered (Patterson, 1983; Rice, 1980), rational emotive (Wessler & Ellis, 1980, 1983), behavioral (Boyd, 1978; Delaney, 1972; Linehan, 1980; Strosahl & Jacobson, 1986), and social learning (Hosford & Barmann, 1983) counseling theories.

Your theoretical counseling orientation, then, will influence to some extent your choice of interventions and your focus during supervision (Friedlander & Ward, 1984; Goodyear, Abadie, & Efros, 1984; Goodyear, Bradley, & Bartlett, 1983; Goodyear & Robyak, 1982; Hart, 1982; Miars et al., 1983; Ward, 1986). You will probably draw from your experience and areas of expertise, and will conceptualize supervision issues in terms similar to your conceptualization of counseling. Your counseling orientation will, for example, influence whether you emphasize the teacher, counselor, or consultant role; the importance you place on the counselor-client and supervisor-supervisee relationships; whether you view supervisees' problems as the result of deficits in learning or as irrational beliefs about themselves, counseling, and/or supervision; whether you "treat" supervisee anxiety with systematic desensitization or explore those feelings in more depth. (See Bartlett, Goodyear, & Bradley, 1983, and Hess, 1980, for more in-depth discussions of theoretically-based supervision interventions.)

There are, however, common threads in the supervision approaches of these theoretical models that are also found in eclectic (e.g., Bernard, 1979; Curtis & Yager, 1981; Martin, Hiebert, & Marx, 1981; Wasik & Fishbein, 1982) and developmental (e.g., Littrell et al., 1979; Loganbill et al., 1982; Stoltenberg, 1981) models of supervision. Most emphasize the modeling of expertise, combine didactic and experiential experiences in supervision, and utilize audio and/or videotapes of counseling sessions, role-plays, and case presentations. Even so, while you will probably use a "common core" of interventions, your supervision style, purpose, and focus will differ somewhat depending on your theoretical orientation.

Supervisor's self-goals. The supervision interventions you choose may also reflect your own learning goals. You may, for example, capitalize on appropriate opportunities to increase your repertoire of specific supervision techniques (e.g., live supervision, IPR, bug-in-the-ear) or to moderate your style (e.g., being more confrontive with the supervisee when needed).

In summary, the needs, preferences, and goals of both the supervisor and the supervisee are taken into consideration in the choice of supervision interventions.

Supervision Interventions

This section will briefly describe some frequently used supervision interventions. (For reviews of research on supervision interventions see Hansen, Pound, & Petro, 1976; Hansen, Robins, & Grimes, 1982; Kaplan, 1983; Lambert, 1980; Matarazzo, 1978; Russell, Crimmings, & Lent, 1984). Most can be adapted to your theoretical orientation and your supervisee's individual needs.

Self-report. Supervisees may report verbally on their own behavior, thoughts, and feelings during a session, their client's responses, and counselor-client interactions. Researchers, however, have found supervisee self-reports to be unreliable, tending to include only material the supervisee is conscious of already, and typically presenting the supervisee in the best possible light (Conver, 1944; Porter, 1950; Walker, 1977). Like all of us, supervisees are limited in their ability to make objective self-observations and unbiased self-evaluations (Hart, 1982).

The supervisee's perceptions of self, client, or the counseling interaction, however, can still provide valuable information (Hart, 1982). Comparing a self-report to the actual session, for example, may reveal "blind spots" and suggest areas to focus on during supervision. To be able to identify such discrepancies, the supervisor can use audio or videotapes, live observation or live supervision.

Audio and videotapes. Audio and videotapes of the counseling session may be used in a variety of ways during the supervision session (Hart, 1982). You may, for example, ask the supervisee to pre-select portions of the tape that illustrate attempts to implement specific goals (e.g., confronting client, use of thought-stopping), periods of counselor confusion or client resistance, and examples of effective interventions. It is helpful to listen to and/or observe opening, middle, and closing portions of the tape to get an overview of the entire process of the counseling session. Tapes can be used to focus on the supervisee's performance skills or cognitive counseling skills (i.e., the rationale and intention for the supervisee's actions), the verbal and nonverbal behavior of both the counselor and client, and the relationship and interaction between the counselor-client.

Smith's (1984) dual channel approach is an innovative use of stereo audiotaping in supervision. Counseling sessions are recorded on one channel while the supervisor's concurrent comments are recorded on another channel. The moment-to-moment feedback on the process of the session augments more general postsession supervision feedback. Hamatz (1975) describes a similar approach, with the supervisor recording comments on the videotape of the session while observing it. Another method is to record comments on a separate tape while reviewing a recording of a counseling session (Dyer & Vriend, 1977).

Structured approaches using audio and videotapes include microtraining and Interpersonal Process Recall (IPR).

Microtraining. Microtraining is a systematic approach to skill acquisition developed by Ivey and his associates (Forsyth & Ivey, 1980; Ivey, 1971; Ivey & Authier, 1978.) A number of studies have demonstrated its efficacy in teaching helping skills; other research has suggested transfer of learning occurs with follow-up training and reinforcement (Forsyth & Ivey, 1980; Ivey, 1980; Ivey & Authier, 1978; Matarazzo, 1978). Originally designed to train novice counselors, more advanced skills have been added to the microtraining paradigm.

In the microtraining approach, identifiable skills (e.g., open questions, reflections of feeling, confrontation) are isolated and taught one at a time. Each skill is presented in a step-by-step procedure that combines several teaching methods: lecture and written manuals describing the skill, observation of videotape models, practice and self-observation using audio or videotapes, peer and supervisor feedback.

The microtraining approach, then, is an especially appropriate supervision intervention for a supervisee who has a specific skill deficit. In addition, Greenberg (1980) has developed a method of training in Gestalt techniques that follows the microtraining approach.

Interpersonal Process Recall (IPR). IPR was developed by Kagan and his associates (Kagan, 1975, 1980; Kagan & Krathwohl, 1967; Kagan, Krathwohl, & Farquhar, 1965; Kagan, Krathwohl, & Miller, 1963) to stimulate the recollections of thoughts and feelings during a counseling session. It has proved effective in improving interviewing and helping skills of counselors, teachers, paraprofessionals, and medical students; it may also facilitate client growth (Kagan, 1980).

IPR materials and training films demonstrate specific procedures for reviewing a videotaped counseling session. In one approach to this "recall session," an "inquirer" (supervisor) debriefs a client by encouraging him/her to stop the videotape and discuss unexpressed feelings, thoughts, and perceptions; the counselor reviews an audiotape of the recall session before meeting with the supervisor. The inquirer may also conduct recall sessions with the counselor alone or with the client and counselor together (mutual recall). These IPR procedures help supervisees better understand themselves, their clients, and the counselor-client relationship.

The inquirer role is facilitative and nonjudgmental, yet confronting and assertive at the same time (Kagan, 1980). By asking questions such as "What pictures, memories, or words were going through your mind?", "How did you want the other person to perceive you?", "How do you think the other person perceived you?", "Was there anything you wanted to say but couldn't find the 'appropriate' words?", and "What would have been the risk in saying what you wanted to say?", the supervisor/inquirer focuses attention on the cognitive and affective aspects of the client and counselor. Questions can be worded to increase supervisees' awareness of their particular blind spots at their own level of readiness and capability. Supervisees may also be taught the inquirer role so that IPR procedures can be used in peer supervision.

Modeling. Modeling approaches have been found effective in teaching basic helping skills, especially when combined with focused feedback (Akamatsu, 1980). Live audio and videotaped models are frequently used to demonstrate specific skills in sequential steps, followed by guided rehearsal of the skill and supervisor reinforcement (Hosford & Barmann, 1983). The supervisor, however, also serves as both an overt and subtle model during each moment of the supervision session.

You may deliberately model, for example, a specific skill, the procedure of a technique, or the follow-up processing of an experiential exercise. But you are also modeling counseling skills when you help a supervisee establish goals and generate alternative counseling interventions, challenge the supervisee to try new approaches, reward risk-taking, and celebrate successes. Less obvious but equally significant is your modeling of professional and ethical behavior (e.g., respect for ethnic and racial diversity, confidentiality), an accepting and congruent attitude, immediacy, self-awareness, and openness to feedback. In addition, supervisors of novice counselors need to be aware that they may be "modeling" more teaching than counseling behaviors, and observe whether their supervisees use these behaviors appropriately with their clients.

Role-playing. Evidence for the utility of role-playing for learning counseling skills has been positive; transfer of learning to the counseling session is enhanced by using realistic role-play situations (Akamatsu, 1980).

Role-playing offers a supervisee several learning opportunities (Hart, 1982). When assuming the client role, supervisees can, for example, (a) observe the supervisor model an intervention, (b) experience the client's response to an intervention, and (c) take on the client's frame of reference to better understand the client's perception of a problem situation, the client's emotions about that situation, or even the client's resistance to change. In the counselor role, supervisees can (a) rehearse a new skill or intervention, (b) practice responding to different types of clients (e.g., resistant, angry, dependent, suicidal, or seductive clients), (c) replay puzzling portions of a session and try new responses, and (d) get immediate feedback from the supervisor about their performance.

Variations of role-playing may be especially helpful for the counselor who reports client resistance or is having difficulty relating to the client effectively (Strosahl & Jacobson, 1986). In a role reversal, the supervisor takes on the role of the counselor while the counselor as client argues against change; in the devil's advocate approach, the supervisor presents the client's perspective on change or the counseling relationship.

You may plan specific role-plays based on your assessment and observations of the supervisee and/or be alert to potential situations during the supervision session that could be clarified through role-playing. Consider your purpose and goal before you assign roles. For example, does the supervisee need to practice explaining the empty-chair exercise to the client, or does the supervisee need to experience the client's response to ineffective confrontation?

Live observation and live supervision. In most training and educational sites, there are one or two-way mirrors that enable the supervisor to observe counseling sessions as they occur. The use of live observation has advantages over reviewing audio and videotapes both in terms of timeliness and sensory input. Supervisory feedback can be given immediately following the session, aiding in the recall of feelings, perceptions, and process interactions (Birchler, 1975; Coppersmith, 1980; Kempster & Savitsky, 1967; Liddle & Halpin, 1978). In addition, supervisees feel more attended to when their counseling sessions are observed live. Worthington (1984) surveyed 237 supervisees from 10 graduate programs in eight states and found that supervisees gave higher ratings to supervisors who frequently employed live observation. The supervisor behind the mirror can also process an ongoing session with other supervisees.

More recently, live supervision has gained popularity among supervisors. Live supervision differs from live observation in that there is the assumption that the supervisor will intervene to redirect the counseling session. There are different methods of accomplishing the task of live supervision. Some supervisors interrupt the counselor only as needed, while other supervisors prefer the counselor leave the room at approximately the same time each session (e.g., after 20 minutes) to discuss the session with the supervisor. Some supervisors prefer a "team" approach where the supervisor and the counselor's fellow supervisees observe the session together and offer interventions as needed, emphasizing learning both from behind the mirror and in their own counseling relationships. Regardless of the particular approach, the advantage of live supervision is that it "eliminates a mutually frustrating situation when the supervisor sees a critical error made by the therapist in the session but must wait until later to tell the therapist—when it is too late to do anything about it!" (Bernard, 1981, pp. 744-745).

After determining a schedule for interrupting counseling sessions, you can choose the method you prefer. One way to intervene is to use the "bug-in-the-ear" method (Baum & Lane, 1976; Boylston & Tuma, 1972) where supervisees wear a small radio receiver in their ear similar to that worn by television anchorpersons or sportscasters. Other methods of contacting the supervisee include the use of a telephone intercom system, or simply knocking on the door to bring the counselor out of the room. Research on the procedures of live supervision is limited (McClure & Vriend, 1976; Tentoni & Robb, 1977), but there are some indications that any interruptions of counseling sessions should be brief and concise so that client rapport is not adversely affected. Supervisor instructions should take the form of "directives" that are behaviorally concise, such as "Pursue the wife relationship" or "Reflect the feelings of loss," rather than "You're going in the wrong direction. Try something else."

Interventions for Advanced Supervisees

Because of their higher skill level and more sophisticated needs, advanced supervisees can benefit from additional interventions that allow for more independent functioning and sharing their knowledge with peers.

Spice and Spice (1976), for example, describe a "triadic" method of structuring supervision that seems appropriate for more skilled supervisees. In this approach, three supervisees assume the roles of supervisee, commentator, and facilitator. During the supervision session, the supervisee presents case material, the commentator critiques case conceptualization, and the facilitator focuses on the counselor-client process issues. The three supervisees alternate roles in successive meetings. The supervisor trains participants and coaches their performance in these roles until he/she can gradually become less directly involved. Because this method requires experience, skill, and some sophistication on the part of supervisees, it may be more suitable for advanced counselors or as an adjunct to traditional one-to-one supervision (Russell et al., 1984).

More advanced supervisees also value observing a supervisor model as a co-therapist with one or more of the supervisees' clients (Hart, 1982; Nelson, 1978). The use of dual (Davis & Arvey, 1978) or multiple supervisors (Fink, Allen, & Barak, 1986) who have different counseling theoretical orientations and supervision styles is appropriate for advanced supervisees who can synthesize and integrate varied feedback into their own counseling approach.

Developmental models (e.g., Littrell et al., 1979; Loganbill et al., 1982; Stoltenberg, 1981) indicate advanced supervisees are ready to deal with personal issues affecting their counseling. Discussions of transference and countertransference, for example, are more common at this level (Heppner & Roelhke, 1984; Miars et al., 1983; Reising & Daniels, 1983). Working through parallel process issues or impasses are also appropriate (see Chapter 5). In addition, Sansbury (1982) suggests group supervision techniques such as sculpting the client's relationships, role-playing, role reversals, and "counseling in a circle" (each group member in turn counsels the "client" portrayed by the counselor) for advanced supervisees.

Other approaches reflect the more consultative relationship preferred by advanced counselors. In tandem supervision (Watson, 1973), for example, two equally experienced professionals consult on cases, but neither is designated as the supervisor of the other. Any decisions about the cases remain the responsibility of the counselor working with the client. This approach seems especially appropriate for the "master counselor" (Stoltenberg, 1981) who seeks continued growth through peer consultation.

Interventions for Cognitive Counseling Skills

There are few established approaches to teaching and supervising cognitive counseling skills (Holloway & Wolleat, 1980). Yet more advanced supervisees may need less focus on counseling performance skills and be ready to develop more sophisticated conceptualization counseling skills.

Several of the previously described interventions can be adapted to focus on cognitive processing and decision-making. In the IPR procedure (Kagan, 1980), for example, the supervisor/inquirer can ask questions that focus on the counselor's perceptions of the client, the counselor's assumptions about the client's perceptions of the counselor, rationale for and intentions of the counselor's responses, and evaluations about performance. The self-supervision model (Bernstein et al., 1986) (see Chapter 3) also helps the counselor verbalize the basis for choosing interventions.

Specific instruction in writing case notes, treatment plans, and final case summaries can also teach cognitive skills. Writing case notes, for example, helps a counselor process client observations and the content of an individual session, identify themes and patterns across sessions, and make appropriate plans for future sessions. Similarly, completing treatment plans teaches a counselor how to formulate clinical hypotheses and select appropriate interventions, while writing final case summaries requires the counselor to synthesize and integrate data over the entire case, evaluate client progress, connect interventions with client growth, and project future client functioning.

Presser and Pfost (1985) describe a format for case notes that emphasizes process. Their form includes a brief summary of the session, the counselor's (a) observations and (b) inferences and hypotheses about the client, counselor, and counselor-client interaction, progress made, and plans for future sessions. The authors have found the format helps supervisees learn discrimination skills as they evaluate what data to record, and develops their ability to relate "observations to conceptualizations, conceptualizations to treatment plans, and treatment plans to progress" (p.15). At first supervisees tend to have an almost exclusive focus on the client. With experience and training they begin to include observations and inferences about their own in-session behavior, and then consider reciprocal influence and interactional patterns of the counseling relationship.

Supervisors might also model the strategies they use to formulate a response and conceptualize a client (Hosford & Barmann, 1983), identifying what information they look for and how they look for it (Kurpius, Benjamin, & Morran, 1985). Kurpius et al. (1985), for example, have devised a systematic cognitive self-instruction strategy that teaches counselors to ask and answer questions about the counseling task, guide their performance with self-instructions, use internal dialogue coping skills to deal with frustration or errors, and give themselves positive reinforcement throughout the process. Instruction in the strategy includes a didactic presentation and a live model "thinking aloud" as he/she forms a clinical hypothesis about a videotaped client. "Thinking aloud" as you and your supervisee process client data or a videotape is one method of modeling effective conceptualization skills.

In addition, Hill and her colleagues (Fuller & Hill, 1985; Hill et al., 1983; Hill & O'Grady, 1985) have developed a coding system of 19 intentions (e.g., support, challenge, reinforce change) of counseling interventions and used it in a series of studies with experienced counselors. Asking supervisees to identify their intentions while reviewing a videotape can help them become more aware of their motivations, and examine their interventions and client responses (Hill & O'Grady, 1985).

Structured approaches to teaching cognitive counseling skills have also been developed. Holloway and Wolleat (1980), for example, created the Clinical Assessment Questionnaire (CAQ), a systematic approach to formulating clinical hypotheses. Following five written tasks outlined in the CAQ, counselors form two hypotheses about a client's problems, designate evidence for those hypotheses, and indicate what additional information they would like to have about the client. Scoring criteria for the CAQ include the elements (e.g., behavior, inferential personal characteristics) and time frames used in understanding the client, categories used to support conclusions (e.g., client statements, body and vocal expressions, counselor-client relationship), the number of facts used to support conclusions, categories of information sought (e.g., client's family history, relationships, attitudes, goals), and the number of divergent questions asked.

Kurpius et al. (1985) have designed a strategy derived from the CAQ to teach counselors how to select and use client information when forming a clinical hypothesis. Counselors are asked to identify (a) the client's major problem or theme, (b) significant internal and external factors about the client, (c) the connection between the internal and external factors, (d) possible cognitive, affective, and behavioral aspects of the client's problem, and (e) the extent to which each of these is related to the problem.

A similiar instrument is the Written Treatment Planning Simulation (WTPS) (Scofield, 1981), designed to evaluate clinical problem solving (Butcher & Scofield, 1984; Butcher, Scofield, & Baker, 1984, 1985). Counselors are asked to design treatment plans for two clients, one inpatient and one outpatient, who are representative of clients served by community mental health settings. Counselors' treatment plans can be analyzed for content and scored for proficiency (proportion of all possibly useful information included) and efficiency (average usefulness of each element included).

Case conceptualization outlines can also provide needed structure for identifying and integrating client data and then choosing appropriate counseling interventions. Hulse and Jennings (1984), for example, have described nine client assessment categories (i.e., expectations, motivation, maturity level, cognitions, behavior, affect, environment, health, cummunication patterns) and possible relationships among them in a Visual Integrative Technique. They suggest introducing the content categories at the prepracticum level, discussing integration of the categorical content at the practicum level, and applying the technique from the perspectives of different theoretical orientations at the advanced level.

Loganbill and Stoltenberg (1983) have also outlined a comprehensive case conceptualization format and suggest using it as a teaching tool with practicum students. The format helps a supervisee combine objective information (e.g., demographics, relevant history, presenting problem) and the supervisee's subjective impressions (e.g., interpersonal style, cognitive functioning, common themes and patterns) into an integrated understanding of the client. The authors report the format has helped their supervisees "in organizing data, clarifying relationships among factors, and developing intervention strategies" (p. 240).

Group Supervision

Many supervisors also work with groups of supervisees, either exclusively or in addition to individual supervision. In a review of the literature from 1960 to 1983, Holloway and Johnston (1985) reported few descriptions of group supervision and even fewer empirical studies of its effectiveness. They did find, however, that most references to group supervision approaches included attention to the three components of case presentation, didactic information, and interpersonal dynamics of the group, and most emphasized the importance of peer support and feedback. In contrast to the interpersonal process groups of the 1960's, more recent approaches separate counseling and supervision functions, discussing counselor dynamics only as they relate to professional role and performance (Holloway & Johnston, 1985). Rioch, Coulter, and Weinberger (1976) provide a rich description of one seminar supervision group focused on the counselor-client relationship that encouraged personal growth only as a desirable by-product.

Several group supervision formats also reflect a developmental framework (e.g., Fraleigh & Buchheimer, 1969; Sansbury, 1982; Yogev, 1982), suggesting supervisors need to adjust content and instructional approaches to the developmental level of the supervisees (Holloway & Johnston, 1985). Group meetings with beginning supervisees would, for example, include didactic presentations, role-plays of intake sessions, and discussions of evaluation procedures and criteria (Yogev, 1982). Novice supervisees would also have the opportunity to recognize the similarity of their feelings and concerns, thus helping meet their critical needs for support (Yogev, 1982). For more advanced supervisees, peer groups would provide opportunities to develop independence through discussions of different perceptions of the counselor-client interaction and the modeling of unique counseling styles (Fraleigh & Buchheimer, 1969). In addition, the supervisor might help the group focus on more sophisticated dynamics, such as members' attitudes and sensitivity toward particular clients or the re-creation of counselor-client issues between group members and the counselor or the supervisor (Sansbury, 1982).

Many of the interventions previously described in this chapter are also appropriate for group supervision, including review of audio and videotapes, role-playing, role reversals, modeling, IPR, live observation and live supervision, and Sansbury's (1982) suggestions for advanced counselors. In addition, Wilbur et al. (1986) outline a structured approach specific to the group setting that encourages feedback from all group members. Following the steps of their model, a supervisee makes a specific request for help, other members ask questions and give suggestions in several round robin procedures, and, following a "structured pause," the supervisee responds to each member's feedback.

Although there is very little empirical support for the efficacy of group supervision, so that it is "widely practiced but poorly understood," Holloway and Johnston (1985) remark on its "intuitive appeal" and believe it will continue to be used extensively by supervisors. You will probably have an opportunity, then, to explore the unique aspects of the group approach to supervision.

Summary

In this chapter you have been introduced to a sample of supervision approaches you may employ with beginning and advanced supervisees to teach performance and cognitive counseling skills in individual and group supervision formats. Through your choice of interventions you are evidencing the creation of your unique style of supervision, a style that is refined and expanded through experience with a variety of supervisees.

Chapter 5

Supervisory Relationship and Process Issues

Several writers have emphasized the pivotal importance of the supervisory relationship for the personal and professional growth of the supervisee (e.g., Ekstein & Wallerstein, 1972; Marshall & Confer, 1980; Moses & Hardin, 1978; Moskowitz & Rupert, 1983; Mueller & Kell, 1972; Patterson, 1983), even describing it as a "working alliance" and "partnership" (Bordin, 1983). The supervisory relationship is viewed as both a vehicle for learning and a significant learning experience itself (Loganbill et al., 1982). Even partnerships, however, are not always congenial, and the supervisory relationship is affected by overt and subtle influences that may interfere with learning. The purpose of this chapter is to describe some typical relationship issues, discuss the conflict inherent in the relationship, and suggest ways to use the supervisory relationship itself as a productive learning experience.

Stage of the Supervisory Relationship

Establishing a supportive environment in the initial supervisory sessions is important from the perspectives of both supervisors (e.g., Blocher, 1983; Hogan, 1964; Littrell et al., 1979; Loganbill et al., 1982; Miars et al., 1983; Stoltenberg, 1981) and beginning and advanced supervisees (e.g., Heppner & Roehlke, 1984; Hutt, Scott, & King, 1983; Rabinowitz et al., 1986; Reising & Daniels, 1983; Worthington & Roehlke, 1979). An open, facilitative relationship develops only with time, however, and, like all relationships, the supervisor-supervisee alliance will inevitably experience conflict during some stages of the relationship (Loganbill et al., 1982; Mueller & Kell, 1972). Ekstein and Wallerstein (1972), for example, use a chess game analogy to describe three stages of the supervisory relationship (opening, mid-game, and end-game), characterizing behavior in the second stage as attacking, defending, probing, and/or avoiding.

Similarly, in Stoltenberg's (1981) developmental model the dependency-autonomy dynamic of the supervisor-supervisee relationship is a theme underlying each stage. As second-level counselors strive to become independent and self-assertive, they can be expected to more frequently disagree with the supervisor about counseling interventions. During the second Confusion stage in Loganbill et al.'s (1982) developmental model, the supervisee experiences (and may express) disappointment and anger upon realizing the supervisor is not the all-knowing, omnipotent person previously perceived. The authors point to the value of the Confusion stage and encourage supervisors to recognize it as a sign of growth and an opportunity for significant new learning.

Variables Influencing the Supervisory Relationship

Supervisory relationships can be influenced by demographic variables and the personalities of the supervisor and supervisee (Bartlett, 1983), affecting supervisees' perceptions of the supervisor, their behaviors during supervision, and their satisfaction with supervision. These influences may be especially critical if one views identification with the supervisor as central to learning (cf., Rubinstein, 1980).

The impact of gender has been investigated by several researchers. Worthington and Stern (1985), for example, reported supervisees perceived closer relationships and attributed more influence to same-gender supervisors, and Rubinstein (1980) found male supervisees expected nurturant behavior from female supervisors but a wider range of behaviors from male supervisors. In addition, Stenack and Dye (1983) observed differential behavior of supervisors with male and female supervisees, and Rubinstein (1980) found male supervisors encouraged imitation and were aware of their impact on supervisees, while female supervisors tended to encourage autonomy and were supportive and nonintrusive.

Sex-role attitudes may also influence the supervision process (Abramowitz & Ambramowitz, 1976; Brodsky, 1980). Brodsky (1980) suggests cross-gender supervision can help both supervisees and supervisors recognize their sex role biases. Race, ethnic, and social class are additional demographic variables that may affect the supervision relationship (Gardner, 1980).

Other possible influences on the supervisory relationship include the supervisor's style (e.g., amount of direction and support, supervision interventions) (Dodds, 1986; Moskowitz & Rupert, 1983), expectations of the relationship (Dodds, 1986), cross-cultural differences (Bartlett, 1983), skill level, and values (Russell et al., 1984). In addition, a supervisee in a field placement may find the agency supervisor's goals and motivations for supervision contrast with the university's goals (Dodds, 1986).

Differences in theoretical orientation and personality also can cause difficulties in the supervisory relationship (Dodds, 1986). For example, 10 of the 52 supervisees in one study who reported a major conflict with a supervisor described disagreements about appropriate approaches or techniques with a client (Moskowitz & Rupert, 1983). These difficulties were relatively easy to discuss and resolve, usually ending in an improved relationship. Personality differences were the most frequent type of conflict reported by the supervisees, and these difficulties were the most difficult to resolve.

One might speculate that matching the supervisor and supervisee on these variables would enhance their relationship, but there is conflicting evidence for this hypothesis (Bartlett, 1983; Hansen et al., 1982; Kaplan, 1983; Russell et al., 1984). At this point, an awareness of the possible impact of differences in demographic variables, theoretical orientation, and personality dynamics can at least alert the supervisor to monitor the relationship for potential difficulties based in these differences. The supervisor can then more deliberately intervene to ameliorate any detrimental effects, and even use the differences as learning opportunities for both persons in the relationship.

Supervisee and Supervisor Resistance

The supervisory roles and functions themselves have a somewhat detrimental effect on efforts to create an open and facilitative relationship. The nature of the supervisory relationship necessarily creates hierarchial distance (Hart, 1982) and a power structure (Robiner, 1982), except, perhaps, for the consultative relationships between the advanced supervisee and supervisor-consultant or between peer professional counselors. The supervisor is responsible for and will evaluate the supervisee, and the supervisee's self-esteem and professional career is at least partially dependent on that evaluation. These conditions usually result in supervisee anxiety.

In the vulnerable learner role, the supervisee is understandably anxious about being observed and evaluated. Like their clients, supervisees have both a desire to learn and change and a reluctance to change (Ekstein & Wallerstein, 1972), wanting both to receive and to avoid feedback. In addition, supervisees are asked to take risks in trying new counseling skills, reveal their honest feelings about clients, and face personal issues affecting their performance. They may doubt their counseling abilities or fear there is something wrong with their personalities rather than their skills. Supervisees, then, may perceive personal threats or losses in the supervisory relationship (Kadushin, 1968; Liddle, 1986).

To deal with their anxiety and to protect themselves, supervisees may exhibit resistant behaviors (Bauman, 1972; Dodge, 1982; Gustin, 1958; Gutheil, 1977) such as being overly enthusiastic, self-effacing, submissive, argumentative, aloof, or forgetful during supervision. In addition, supervisees may play "games" such as "Be nice to me because I am nice to you," "I did like I was told," "It's all so confusing," and "What you don't know won't hurt me," in their efforts to maintain control (Kadushin, 1968).

Supervisee resistance, of course, interferes with learning (Bauman, 1972; Kadushin, 1968) so that the supervisor needs to intervene to either (a) reduce the perceived threat or (b) help the supervisee find new coping strategies that do not prohibit learning (Liddle, 1986). Since resistant behavior is a natural and sometimes necessary reaction to change, the supervisor might first ask if the resistance is "useful, helpful, or functional" (Bauman, 1972, p. 254). It is appropriate, for example, for supervisees to resist challenges to perform beyond their capabilities or level of readiness, or as a result of inadequate support from the supervisor (Liddle, 1986).

Other times supervisees may resist changes they are capable of making because of their natural apprehension about risk-taking and evaluative feedback. To reassure supervisees that their anxiety is "normal," videotapes of supervisees describing the sources of their anxieties can be shown to succeeding generations of supervisees (Goodyear, 1985; Yager & Beck, 1985). The videotapes can help supervisees acknowledge their anxieties, demonstrate appropriate and inappropriate responses to them, and reduce their worries about worrying. To reduce evaluation anxiety, supervisors can give specific and clear performance standards (Goodyear & Bradley, 1983), make evaluation less formal (e.g., Arbuckle, 1963; Johnston & Gysbers, 1967; Kelly, 1976), reward risk-taking and improvement (Liddle, 1986), or use cognitive-behavioral interventions (e.g., address supervisees' irrational beliefs about counseling performance and supervision) (e.g., Dodge, 1982; Liddle, 1986; Schmidt, 1979; Wessler & Ellis, 1983). Supervisor self-disclosure may also help reduce anxiety (Williams et al., 1985).

Supervisee resistance may also be based in more personal issues, including feelings about persons in authority or about intimacy in relationships. These resistant behaviors may reflect typical defensive reactions (Bauman, 1972) or established coping strategies such as Kadushin's (1968) games. Suggestions for dealing with this more subtle supervisee resistance include direct approaches such as nondefensive interpretation and confrontation, and indirect approaches such as generalization, ignoring, role-playing, and listening to an audiotape of the supervision session together (Bauman, 1972; Kadushin, 1968; Mueller & Kell, 1972). In addition, Guttman (1973) describes training in nondefensive behavior using a microtraining approach, while Liddle (1986) advocates a mutual problem-solving session during which the supervisor and supervisee identify the sources of anxiety, brainstorm possible ways to reduce the perceived threat, select and implement appropriate actions, and identify outside sources of support and stability (e.g., significant others).

It is important, however, for supervisors to recognize how they also contribute to relationship problems (Langs, 1980). Supervisors may exhibit detrimental behavior as a result of confusion about their multiple roles (Robiner, 1982) or difficulty dealing with their evaluative and authoritative roles (Hawthorne, 1975; Kadushin, 1968), particularly in their first supervision experiences (Styczynski, 1980). In addition, Kadushin (1968) points out that a supervisee can play games only in collusion with a supervisor who also enjoys payoffs from the game, such as flattery and being liked.

Hawthorne (1975) describes additional games supervisors themselves may set up in an attempt to deal with their problems concerning authority. Games of abdication include "They won't let me" and "I'm really one of you"; games of power, "Remember who's boss" and "I know you really can't do it without me." As a result of both types of games, the supervisor's authority is never clarified, yet the supervisory role is retained. Supervisors may also experience counter-resistant feelings toward the supervisee, in effect being determined to resist the supervisee's resistance (Bauman, 1972).

Rozsnafszky (1979) describes caricatures of immature and insecure supervisors who act out of an unconscious need for conquest and power. In contrast to "Teddy Bear," "Fox," "Super Guru," and "Big Mother," mature supervisors "illustrate a genuine understanding of students' and patients' needs, a willingness to tell hard truths with respect, the maturity to face the therapeutic relationship without sexualizing it, and a sense of their own limitations" (p. 198).

In summary, supervisee and supervisor resistance is natural and expected, but detrimental to the learning process. You may intervene rather directly to reduce supervisee anxiety about evaluation. It may take some experience, however, to be able to recognize the more subtle resistant behaviors resulting from the interactions of the two individual personalities involved. As a preventive measure, you may want to consider your thoughts and feelings about your multiple roles and authority position as a supervisor and discuss them with your own supervisor or peers.

Parallel Process

Several authors have pointed to concurrent similarities in the dynamics of the counselor-client relationship and the supervisor-supervisee relationship. They have described several types of "parallel processes" that impact learning during supervision.

The "reflection process" (Searles, 1955) refers to the supervisee unconsciously behaving like the client in an effort to communicate subtle client dynamics to the supervisor. Unable to verbally express all his/her perceptions of the client, the supervisee "acts out" in an attempt to evoke in the supervisor the same feelings he/she experienced with the client (Hora, 1957). A panicked client, for example, demands the counselor tell him what to do; caught up in the client's affect, the overwhelmed counselor turns to the supervisor for a quick solution to the client's dilemma. In response to the counselor's behavior, the supervisor feels an urgent need to take over or provide an answer. The supervisor who is alert to the reflection process, however, can interrupt the spiraling affective reactions and, instead, point out the message the client seems to be trying to convey through his behavior. Searles (1955) suggests supervisors be aware that their personal reactions to supervisees may offer valuable information about the counselor-client relationship, and cautions against being critical of a supervisee's counseling ability on the basis of the presentation of the case.

Other "parallel re-enactments" of impasses in the counselor-client relationship can result from client resistance, counselor feelings of inadequacy, and inappropriate counselor identification with the client ("I can't help this client because I have the same problem") (Mueller & Kell, 1972). In addition, supervisees' "problems about learning" in supervision and their "learning problems" with counseling may be the result of similar transference and countertransference issues in the two relationships (Ekstein & Wallerstein, 1958). Parallel impasses in the supervisor-supervisee relationship can become a source of growth as the supervisor models how to respond therapeutically to conflict (Moldawsky, 1980; Mueller & Kell, 1972). Instruction in techniques is an insufficient supervisory intervention for these issues; instead, the supervisory relationship itself becomes a vehicle for learning about the dynamics of the counseling relationship (Ekstein & Wallerstein, 1958).

Doerhman (1976) has described additional, multiple levels of the parallel process. The results of her study indicate the "reflection process" works in more than one direction: counselors in her study also "played supervisor" with their clients, behaving with clients in the same or opposite ways they perceived their supervisors behaving toward them. Both positive and negative behaviors during supervision were observed during counseling, and resolution of transference impasses in the supervisory relationship were closely followed by resolution of transference binds in the counseling relationship. The parallel process phenomenon was also observed in counselors' relationships with other supervisors, their own therapists, and the researcher. More recently, Martin, Goodyear, and Newton (1986) have speculated a supervisor's work with one supervisee could influence what is happening with another supervisee, thus constituting another form of parallel process.

Psychotherapists responding to a survey of their experiences with parallel process described instances of their supervisors and themselves avoiding the same issues in supervision (Aldrich & Hess, 1983). Sexuality, authority conflicts, and evaluation anxiety were the most frequently mentioned issues, and the respondents reported these experiences as negative. When reporting on their experiences as supervisors, however, they described instances of parallel process more positively and tended to view them as learning opportunities.

Recognition of the carry-over effects of a supervisee's identification with the client and/or supervisor is an awareness supervisors need to cultivate. Working through conflict, impasses, or transference binds in the supervisory relationship first can be a potent learning experience, increasing supervisees' understanding of relationship dynamics and serving as a powerful model for working therapeutically through the counseling relationship (Doehrman, 1976; Hora, 1957; Searles, 1955).

Summary

Numerous mediating factors influence the supervisory relationship and the learning process, and, as a result, conflict is fairly typical in supervisory relationships (Moskowitz & Rupert, 1983). Dealing with these conflicts as they occur is crucial (Moskowitz & Rupert, 1983), as is the recognition that both the supervisee and supervisor contribute to relationship problems (Langs, 1980). Supervisees want the supervisor to openly identify and discuss the relationship problem (Moskowitz & Rupert, 1983). Unresolved conflicts interfere with the learning experience, causing supervisees to exhibit self-protective behaviors (Rosenblatt & Mayer, 1975). It is the supervisor's responsibility to be alert to relationship problems and to initiate discussion of them so that learning opportunities are not impaired.

Chapter 6

Evaluation of the Supervisee

Evaluation of the supervisee is often the sole responsibility of the individual supervisor (Trent & Galassi, 1986; Tyler & Weaver, 1981). Evaluation includes verbal feedback during each supervision session, and verbal and written feedback at specified intervals such as the mid-point and end of the semester. While the importance of evaluation to the supervisee's efforts to change and improve is obvious, many supervisors find giving feedback uncomfortable, and often have not received training in evaluation skills (Cormier & Bernard, 1982; Goodyear & Bradley, 1983). Even though supervisees are inevitably anxious about being evaluated (see Chapter 5), they want feedback and value supervisors who give direct, impartial, and thorough evaluations that reflect respect for the supervisee as a person (Allen et al., 1986; Worthington & Roehlke, 1979). Evaluation is also a supervisor's ethical responsibility (see Chapter 7).

This chapter outlines guidelines to help you give verbal and written feedback that will positively contribute to the supervisory relationship and your supervisee's growth.

Feedback during Supervision Sessions

You took the first step for giving effective feedback in your initial sessions when you established a working relationship and specified the criteria and procedures for evaluation. The supervisor who communicates warmth, respect, genuineness, and positive regard will create a relationship in which the supervisee feels accepted rather than threatened and can be open rather than defensive. In this environment the supervisee can "hear" straightforward feedback and challenges to risk and grow; the supervisor's main task can then be to monitor the balance of challenge and support in the learning environment (Blocher, 1983).

Feedback with a behavioral rather than a personal focus can increase the supervisee's receptivity to an effective use of feedback (Loganbill et al.,

47

1982; Turock, 1980). Turock (1980) suggests a supervisor point to the presence or absence of specific, concrete behaviors, describe the client's response to these behaviors, and suggest alternative behaviors. Worthington (1984) advises supervisors to frame the question, "Did that intervention facilitate or impede your goal?" When feedback follows these guidelines, the supervisor avoids making global judgments and labeling, and the supervisee is less likely to hear personal criticism.

Feedback is also more effective if it is directly related to the short and long-term goals and action plan for supervision. Any improvement toward these goals needs to be rewarded (Forsyth & Ivey, 1980) so that the supervisee can experience the success that will fuel work toward new goals. You can also encourage the supervisee to restate feedback and to ask for clarification to be sure it is understood and can be successfully employed.

Being challenged, however, is also crucial to the development to the supervisee. These more confrontive statements point out discrepancies between actual performance and mastery level criteria for counseling skills (Turock, 1980), between exposed theory and actual behavior (Forsyth & Ivey, 1980), and between supervisee feelings and behavior (Loganbill et al., 1982). For example, a supervisee may maintain a belief in client responsibility for problems and change, yet allow clients to list all the reasons they "can't" behave differently, or continually try to problem-solve for clients. In addition, a supervisee may not be able to recognize or accept angry feelings toward a client although you perceive these feelings in nonverbal behavior and indirect critical, judging responses. Confrontive feedback may also point to differences between the supervisor's and supervisee's perceptions of the client (Loganbill et al., 1982). The supervisee, for example, seeks input to help a couple "save their marriage," yet the couple's flat affect and "yes, but's" indicate their lack of commitment to compromise and change.

Although "confrontation" often has a negative connotation, it can be a positive challenge (Loganbill et al., 1982). Egan (1986), for example, describes confrontation as an invitation to examine and change ineffective behavior. Guidelines for making constructive challenges include (a) keeping the goal in mind (i.e., help the supervisee clarify or develop new perspectives rather than express your annoyance with the supervisee), (b) allowing for self-challenge (i.e., "I wonder if..." or two-chair exercise), and (c) earning the right to challenge (i.e., establishing the relationship first and being open to challenge yourself). Effective challenging statements (a) are tentative (i.e., "I wonder if...", "How does this fit for you?"), (b) include a sense of caring and respect, (c) build on successes, (d) are concrete and specific (i.e., pointing to behaviors and their consequences rather than the person), and (e) challenge strengths rather than weaknesses, helping the supervisee identify assets, resources, positive behaviors and attitudes they can use to make changes. Examples of constructive confrontation include the following:

You say you believe in helping the client generate alternatives, yet you've made five suggestions without ever asking her what she's tried before or what ideas she has for changing her behavior. How can you change your behavior to make it match what you want to do, to help the client come up with her own alternatives?

With your other clients you have easily established rapport. But here I notice both you and the client are sitting rigidly, and you've pushed your chair back several times. What's different in this session with this client that you aren't using your facilitative skills?

You asked me to focus on this client's resistant behavior, and you've pointed out the nonverbal behaviors and "yes, but" statements that indicate resistance. Let's watch the videotape again, and this time use your observational skills to identify and describe your nonverbal and verbal responses.

"Confrontive techniques" are also described within each theoretical orientation, and you can adapt those you prefer for working with your supervisee. In a role reversal, for example, the supervisee can experience the client's affective response to the counselor's continuous use of questions, while the use of Gestalt approaches can facilitate supervisee self-awareness.

Formal Evaluation

In addition to the ongoing specific feedback during sessions, supervisees need more comprehensive mid-point and final evaluations of their performance. The mid-point assessment provides an opportunity to summarize progress and identify areas for additional work, and, if needed, restate learning goals and the working contract. The final evaluation summarizes growth in skills and developmental issues, encourages the supervisee to acknowledge what they already know, and sets the stage for new goals and the next action plan.

Many supervisors provide written formal evaluations (Tyler & Weaver, 1981), an approach that is useful for record-keeping and constructive discussion with the supervisee. Written evaluations may include unstructured descriptions of supervisee behaviors or characteristics and/or standardized ratings scales (Tyler & Weaver, 1981). You may also ask the supervisee to write a summary statement based on the initial goal statement and/or complete the same rating scale you are using as a basis for mutual discussion. In addition, client feedback on an open-ended evaluation questionnaire (e.g., This counselor helped me..., This counselor could have better helped me by...) or standardized rating scales (for examples see the next section), will add an important perspective. Lambert (1980) advocates such an approach that solicits feedback from several sources.

Objective evaluation scales. Choice of an objective instrument for your final assessment of the supervisee will depend on the purpose of the evaluation, your theoretical orientation and definition of counseling effectiveness, and the stage of supervisee development (Goodyear & Bradley, 1983; Trent & Galassi, 1986). Published scales differ in who serves as the rater (e.g., supervisor, counselor, client, observer), whether the focus is the counseling or supervision session (Holloway, 1984; Lambert, 1980), and the theoretical base of the scale (Ponterotto & Furlong, 1985).

Some instruments and procedures to assess supervisees' performance skills, cognitive counseling skills, and developmental level have been described in previous chapters (see Chapters 2, 3, 4). The use of the same evaluation tool as a posttest can provide specific feedback on changes and progress toward goals (cf., Holahan & Galassi, 1986). Materials accumulated in the supervisee's portfolio (Atkinson & Zimmer, 1977) will also provide concrete evidence of growth.

Evaluation of counseling performance skills may include frequency counts of counselor behaviors using the Hill Counselor Verbal Response Category System (Hill, 1978) or ICB (Dustin et al., 1982), comparison of ratings of facilitative skills completed by initial and later clients or by the supervisor. Other instruments designed to rate counselor effectiveness include the Counselor Evaluation Inventory (Linden, Stone, & Shertzer, 1965), a measure of counseling climate, counselor comfort, and client satisfaction, and the Counselor Effectiveness Scale (Ivey, 1971; Ivey & Authier, 1978), a general measure of counselor effectiveness. In addition, three instruments are designed to measure counselor influence (expertness, attractiveness, trustworthiness): Counselor Rating Form (Barak & LaCrosse, 1975), Counselor Rating Form-Short Version (Corrigan & Schmidt, 1983), and Counselor Effectiveness Rating Scale (Atkinson & Wampold, 1982). Although developed primarily to be used by the client (Ponterroto & Furlong, 1985), these instruments could also be completed by the supervisor, counselor, or an observer. Supervisors can use an additional instrument, the Counselor Evaluation Rating Scale (Myrick & Kelly, 1971) to evaluate a supervisee's behavior during both counseling and supervision sessions. Other scales are included in Boyd (1978) and Dimick and Krause (1980); Boyd also provides an annotated listing of rating instruments.

The supervisee can demonstrate level of competency in cognitive counseling skills by writing a comprehensive case conceptualization (e.g., Hulse & Jennings, 1984; Loganbill & Stoltenberg, 1983), writing a final summary report about the client, or completing the CAQ (Holloway & Wolleat, 1980) or WTPS (Butcher et al., 1985) (see Chapter 4). Other indications of competency are the inclusion of more sophisticated counseling dynamics (e.g., counselor-client interactional patterns) in case notes (Presser & Pfost, 1985) and effective use of the self-supervision model (Bernstein & Lecomte, 1979) (see Chapters 3 and 4).

Supervisee developmental growth can be assessed by administering the Supervisee Levels Questionnaire (McNeill et al., 1985) or the Supervision Level Scale (Wiley & Ray, 1986) as a posttest (see Chapter 2). Completing the assessment chart based on the Loganbill et al. (1982) (Figure 5) model can indicate stage growth for each supervisory issue (e.g., competence, emotional awareness, professional identity).

Reviewers of training and supervision research suggest client outcome is also a crucial criteria for evaluating counselor's learning and the effectiveness of their behaviors with clients (Hansen et al., 1976; Holloway, 1984; Lambert, 1980; Matarazzo, 1978). In a comprehensive review of supervision outcome measures, however, Holloway (1984) found no scales for the supervisor, counselor, client, or observer to evaluate client behavior. Despite the lack of instrumentation, however, you can give some attention to the progress made by your supervisee's clients in your final evaluation.

Assigning a Grade

Some practica and internships are evaluated on pass/fail competency-based criteria; others require a letter or number grade. The criteria you specified in the initial session will serve as the guideline for grading, such as what percentages of the grade are based on performance of counseling skills, improvement of skills, paperwork (e.g., case notes, final summary reports), professional and ethical behavior, relationships with staff at the practicum or internship site, and any additional assignments (see Chapter 3). The actual grade can be discussed during the supervision session along with the formal evaluation summary.

Summary

Evaluative feedback is critical to a supervisee's learning. Supportive and challenging feedback facilitate learning during the semester; final evaluations help supervisees consolidate learning, determine "what's next," and make goals and plans for continued growth.

Chapter 7

Ethical and Legal Considerations for Supervisors

Janine M. Bernard

The late 1970's and the 1980's have brought a dual focus to the counseling profession: a substantial increase of interest in the area of ethics as evidenced by new books, special issues of journals and numerous articles, and a heightened awareness of the legal responsibilities inherent in the helping professions. Although these two thrusts are not necessarily related (i.e., although one may be guilty of no ethical violation, one may still fall victim to unjust litigation), the two are usually paired.

Hopefully, the profession's interest in ethics does not stem from its fear of legal consequences if ethics are overlooked. Tennyson and Strom (1986) make the point that ethics themselves can be approached legalistically in a letter of the law fashion. In contrast, the authors challenge counseling professionals to aspire to "responsibleness" rather than the more confining concept of responsibility. They imply that ethics should be the beginning, not the end. This distinction between ethical and legal considerations must be underlined: the law looks for the least common denominator when evaluating a situation and determining whether negligence can be determined: ethics, though they often are presented as minimal standards, include the assumption that they will be used as cornerstones to be built upon. Ethical standards do not, nor can they, address every situation (Mabe & Rollin, 1986). Therefore, ethical standards will always call for interpretation, expansion, and professional integrity from those who adhere to them.

Each supervisor continually makes choices as to whether he/she will adhere to the legalistic least common denominator or aspire to the highest ethical standard. Furthermore, the supervisor engages in this process with the awareness that one is always vulnerable to litigation regardless of one's standards of professional behavior (although it is unlikely that a determination of negligence will be made); conversely, most unethical behavior or substandard behavior remains untouched or undetected by the legal establishment.

The following is a list of ethical/legal themes of which you as a supervisor need to be cognizant. Most of these are given more detailed attention elsewhere (e.g., Cormier & Bernard, 1982; Newman, 1981; Stadler, 1986; Upchurch, 1985; Van Hoose & Kottler, 1977). Issues may focus on the supervisor/counselor relationship, supervisor/client relationship, the relationship between the supervisor and the profession, or all three.

Dual Relationship

The topic of dual relationship has been given most extensive coverage in the professional literature. This is due, most likely, to the tremendous abuse of the therapy situation by therapists who have had sexual relations with clients. However, there are at least three types of possible dual relationships between supervisor and counselor: (a) there is a dual relationship if the supervisor and the counselor are involved sexually; (b) if the supervisor becomes the counselor's therapist, a dual relationship has been formed; and (c) a degree of closeness separate from sexual contact *could* evolve into a dual relationship.

The first of these is clear-cut. There seems to be no defensible argument for the ethics of sexual involvement between supervisor and supervisee. This does not mean that in a training situation where counselors and supervisors may be chronological peers that intimate relationships do not occur. When such an involvement emerges, however, it is imperative that the counselor receive a new supervisor or an additional supervisor to insure that the counselor is supervised and evaluated objectively. It goes without saying that supervisors are responsible for seeing that their supervisees are not engaging in sexual relationships with their clients.

The next two types of dual relationships involve "grey" areas. Some models of supervision expect the supervisor to be in the therapist role. Others see insight or personal growth on the part of the supervisee as the primary goal of supervision. Therefore, in these instances, a dual role would not be resultant. However, if the supervisor experiences a dual role, one of therapist and one of supervisor, duality probably exists and steps should be taken to remove one of the two roles.

Finally, the colleagial relationships that sometimes develop between counselor and supervisor should be monitored to avoid a third type of dual relationship. Often persons working together who have a good deal in common become close personal friends. When the relationship makes objective assessment extremely difficult or impossible, a dual relationship has evolved. It is not always imperative to remove a supervisor in this case, but, at the very least, outside consultation should be sought by the supervisor to affirm that his or her evaluation of the supervisee is accurate.

Due Process

Due process issues between supervisor and counselor have to do with the parameters of the supervision experience. The counselor should know what is expected of him/her to do well (in a course or in employment). For instance, relating to the discussion above, if the supervisor adheres to a "personal growth" model of supervision, the supervisee should be aware of this and be in basic agreement with the model's tenets. The supervisor must monitor the counselor's progress closely and must offer some form of intervention if the counselor is not performing well. In other words, the supervisor *must supervise* or the counselor's due process rights have been violated. Finally, feedback should be given periodically and not only at the end of the supervisory relationship, and this feedback should include something in writing that both parties sign.

Evaluation

The *form* of evaluation is a due process issue; the *fact* of evaluation is an ethical responsibility the supervisor has to the counselor, the profession, and to future clients of the supervisee. Supervisors have an ethical responsibility to screen out those counselors who do not have adequate skills to perform competently. In addition, supervisors must be clear about articulating their supervisees' weaknesses at the end of supervision. For instance, an "A" in a beginning practicum rarely means that the counselor is prepared to go into private practice.

Informed Consent

By virtue of supervision, the supervisor has a relationship with the client through the counselor. It is necessary that the client be informed of that relationship and all its dimensions. If supervision means that the client is being observed during sessions, he/she must know that. Similarly, the client must be aware that a tape of a session may be viewed or heard by a group of students with the supervisor if that is indeed the case. In addition, the client must be cognizant that the counseling relationship may be a time-limited one, and, in some instances, may have certain limits regarding confidentiality. Furthermore, the parameters of supervision and the counseling relationship should be revealed to the client before the establishment of a counseling relationship. It is the supervisor's implied responsibility to see that the client is so informed.

Confidentiality

Confidentiality has become an increasingly more complicated concept for the helping professions. Ethics and the law have merged over this issue and counselors must be taught when to break confidentiality as well as when to uphold it. Corey, Corey, and Callanan (1984) include an excellent section in their book on the topic of confidentiality and outline many of the guidelines that are imperative for counselors and supervisors to incorporate in their work (pp. 170-188). For supervisors, it is critical to be aware of cases where the issue of confidentiality is in question. *Not knowing* about the specifics of a case is not a defensible position, as was clearly demonstrated by the Tarasoff v. the Regents of the University of California case (see Cormier & Bernard, 1982). The issue of supervisor awareness leads to the next topic, vicarious liability.

Vicarious Liability

The Tarasoff case heightened the profession's awareness of what has been referred to as vicarious liability (Cohen, 1979). "According to this doctrine, someone in a position of authority or responsibility, such as a supervisor, is responsible for acts of his or her trainees or assistant. Stated another way, supervisors are ultimately legally responsible for the welfare of clients counseled by their supervisees" (Cormier & Bernard, 1982, p. 488).

It is important to note that this is more a legal issue than an ethical one. Ethically, it may be sound to trust a particular counselor's ability to alert you if a case needs additional scrutiny. If circumstances lead to litigation, however, the supervisor is liable if he/she was unaware of any critical aspects of the counseling situation. Ironically, if the supervisor is aware of the case, but makes an incorrect judgment regarding the case, he/she probably will not be found to be liable. The law does not ask the supervisor to be infallible, but rather, to be involved.

Isolation

An additional responsibility of a supervisor is to avoid isolation from peers. Supervision is a serious activity and one with unforeseen challenges. It is important that a supervisor has a network of colleagues, "a place to go" for consultation when needed in order to meet the complex demands of supervision.

Training for Ethical Supervision

Assuming that a supervisor is well equipped for the practice of supervision, the use of role-play is a most efficient way to sensitize oneself (with a group of peers or supervisees) to potential ethical dilemmas. I have found that it is best to have a group come up with their own examples of real or hypothetical situations and role-play (or brainstorm) solutions. The more tension that can be produced the better, because it will allow the players to learn more about their style in uncomfortable situations. For example, one person could play the part of someone representing a client (legally or otherwise) with a complaint about the counselor, perhaps one of sexual overtures. The supervisor is given partial information which presumably came from the counselor. (The counselor is not in the role play.) Therefore, the supervisor must handle the person in his/her presence without knowing the whole story and possibly doubting for the first time the relationship between him/her and the counselor. The discussion following the role play will allow many issues to surface which can be discussed by the participants.

Because many ethical situations involve miscommunications or incomplete communications, practice at negotiating such instances is important. An example is given at the end of this chapter of a critical incident and how it is constructed to produce tension in a role play. Much can be learned about one's style in such a role play. An excellent additional resource for exercises and stimulus materials dealing with ethical dilemmas is Corey, Corey and Callanan (1984).

Figure 6. Ethical issues: Critical incident.

The following is a very common ethical dilemma for clinical supervisors. For the role play, two people volunteer to play the roles of counselor and supervisor. They are given the information pertaining to their roles only. The rest of the participants (observers) are given descriptions of both roles. Observers should be sensitive to the supervisor's role choice (teacher, consultant, counselor) as she talks to the counselor. (For this role-play, the counselor is male and the supervisor is female.)

Counselor:

You are seeing a female client who has seen another therapist in town. When you ask her if she is currently seeing this person she is vague. You inform her that you must contact her former therapist before you can continue to see her. You call the therapist but she is not in. You make another attempt with the same result. Since then you have made no further attempts to contact the former therapist. There has been no further mention of this therapist in your sessions with your client and you assume that the issue is past. In your most recent counseling session with your client, she talks about being very depressed. You want to talk to your supervisor about the possibility of recommending her to a physician in conjunction with counseling since you believe that her depression is interfering with counseling progress. She has not been sleeping or eating well. This is your major concern as you enter this supervision session. Your supervisor was not able to observe your last session so she is dependent on your self report for supervision.

Supervisor:

One of your counselors is seeing a female client and there is some question whether the client is also seeing another therapist. The counselor informs the client that he must contact the other therapist and the client does not resist. Three weeks later you receive a very cold phone call from the therapist who was to be contacted. She has just learned that her client has been seeing your counselor. She makes clear that professional courtesy (if not ethics) has been violated by your agency since she was not contacted by you or the counselor. You are about to have a supervision session with this counselor concerning his last session with this client. You were not able to observe this session so you will have to rely on self report for supervision purposes. Your most urgent intent, however, is to discuss this breach of professional conduct.

This incident was taken from Bernard, J.M. (1982). A training laboratory in clinical supervision. Unpublished manuscript. Reprinted by permission.

Chapter 8

Evaluation of the Supervisor

An important final step in your first (and all future) experiences as a supervisor is to invite feedback about your skills, style, and development. If you are a doctoral student in a counselor education program, you may have been receiving supervision of your work all along. It is still advisable, however, to schedule an "evaluation session" with your supervisor and ask for a formal verbal and/or written assessment. Your supervisor's feedback will help you evaluate your strengths, identify the areas you have developed, and set goals for your next supervision experience.

The list of learning goals you wrote in Chapter 1 are also useful criteria for evaluation in conjunction with your supervisor and supervisee, or for self-evaluation. You probably achieved some goals and partially achieved others. An overview of your progress may help you identify the areas in which you developed quickly, those goals that were more difficult to accomplish, and those areas that weren't a problem after all. For example, you anticipated you would tend to be verbose and stay in the teacher role; in reality, you found those teaching skills appropriate for your beginning supervisee and also found your counselor's sensitive ears enabled you to smoothly move into a more supportive role at some crucial times. Finally, you probably can add some new goals for areas you had not anticipated would be relevant to the supervisor role or were new personal dynamics you discovered about yourself (e.g., reluctance to give critical feedback, lack of effective methods to deal with supervisee's resistance to audiotaping clients). Also read your description of your anticipated supervision style; you may find you now need to make modifications based on your actual performance.

In addition, there are more formal evaluation instruments you can ask your supervisees or supervisor to complete. Your choice will depend on what skills you believe are crucial to supervision, your goals for yourself as a supervisor, and your purposes for evaluation. One example is Janine M. Bernard's rating scale counselors use to evaluate their supervisors (Figure 7).

Holloway (1984) has identified instruments used in research to evaluate the supervisor, and counselor educators and supervisors have recently developed additional rating forms. The literature includes frequent references to other unpublished rating scales developed for a particular study. The following list, based in part on Holloway's (1984) review, briefly describes some of the more frequently used or recently developed instruments. They vary according to whether they are completed by you, your supervisee, your supervisor, or more than one person, and reflect a variety of theoretical orientations.

1. *Supervisor Questionnaire* (SQ; Worthington & Roehlke, 1979). Supervisees indicate their perceptions of how frequently their supervisors performed a list of behaviors judged as important to good supervision, behaviors that have been related to satisfaction with supervision. The SQ and the revised SQ-R (Worthington, 1984) include behaviors such as giving support, giving direct help, establishing a relationship, and helping supervisees evaluate their own strengths and weaknesses. The SQ has been used in several research studies and adopted as the standard evaluation scale of supervisors by some counselor education programs.

2. *Barrett-Lennard Relationship Inventory* (BLRI; Barrett-Lennard, 1962). The BLRI and the various Carkhuff-type scales are completed by supervisees and evaluate the facilitative skills of the supervisor. Based on Rogers' necessary and sufficient conditions for therapeutic change, the BLRI has five subscales (i.e., level of regard, empathic understanding, congruence, unconditional positive regard, willingness to be known).

3. *Supervision Styles Inventory* (SSI; Friedlander & Ward, 1984). On parallel versions, the supervisor and supervisee use 25 adjectives that positively describe supervision to characterize the supervisor's style. The SSI has yielded three factors: attractive, interpersonally sensitive, and task-oriented.

4. *Supervisor Emphasis Rating Form* (Lanning, 1986). Using parallel forms, the supervisor and supervisee indicate what skills the supervisor focuses on during supervision (e.g., process skills, personalization skills, conceptual skills, and professional behaviors).

5. *Supervisor Rating Form* (SRF; Heppner & Handley, 1981). The SRF is an adaptation of the Counselor Rating Form (Barak & LaCrosse, 1975). Supervisees indicate perceptions of the supervisor's expertness, attractiveness, and trustworthiness.

6. *Supervisor Personal Reaction Scale* (SPRS; Holloway & Wampold, 1983; adapted from the Therapist Personal Reaction Scale, Ashby, Ford, Guerney, & Guerney, 1957). Using a Likert-type scale [1) highly characteristic to 5) not characteristic] for the 32 items, supervisors evaluate their own performance and the supervisees' performance, and indicate their level of comfort in expressing their own ideas. The Trainee Personal Reaction Scale (TPRS) is a parallel version for supervisees.

7. *Supervision Assessment Scale* (Hart, 1982, pp. 249-251). Supervisees indicate the frequency their supervisors made statements focusing on areas such as the client's personality dynamics, counseling techniques, and the supervisee-supervisor relationship. The statements represent Hart's three models of supervision: skill development, personal growth, and integration.

8. *Supervisor Role Analysis* (Gysbers & Johnston, 1965). The supervisee rates a list of supervisor behaviors, giving an opinion of the supervisor's obligation to perform those behaviors [from 1) absolutely must to 5) absolutely must not]. The behaviors seem most relevant to supervisors of school counselors.

9. *Blumberg's Interactional Analysis* (BIA; Blumberg, 1970). Based on Flanders's system for analyzing classroom interaction, the BIA has been used to categorize the supervisor's (and supervisee's) indirect and direct behavior (e.g., asking for counselor's opinion, giving opinion or suggestions).

10. *Competencies of Supervisors* (Figure 8). The ACES Supervision Committee adopted this list of supervisor competencies at the New York AACD Convention in April 1985. The list of competencies, the result of a Delphi survey, includes knowledge and skills relevant to both administrative and counseling supervision. In the list in Figure 6 we have added a rating scale of 1 (needs development) to 5 (expertise area). Not all the competencies may be relevant to your setting, depending on your administrative and counseling supervision responsibilities.

Whether you ask for informal feedback from your supervisee and supervisor, use a formal evaluation instrument, and/or create your own list of supervisor behaviors and attitudes, a post-evaluation of your performance is important personally and professionally. Self-evaluation is also desirable, since the willingness to be self-critical is one component of competent supervision (Alonso, 1983). Inviting feedback, being open to constructive criticism, and modifying your supervision as appropriate is one way to model for your supervisee the desire to grow, even as you do grow and develop your supervision knowledge and skills.

Termination of Supervision

The final supervision session is similar to the termination session with a client, in that it can be an important catalyst for change, not just "the end." Therapeutic termination sessions with clients have three functions: (a) summarizing progress toward goals, (b) discussing how changes will be maintained and identifying the "next steps" for continued growth, and (c) achieving a sense of closure in the relationship (Ward, 1984).

The suggestions in Chapter 6 for the final evaluation of the supervisee include the first two functions. You initiated a dialogue by asking your supervisee for feedback on your performance, and so set up the opportunity to discuss your relationship, the third function of termination.

There is often a need to express more personal feedback in the final session, since both you and the supervisee have invested much time and energy in this learning experience and in your relationship. It is not uncommon, then, for each of you to want to share reflections about your interactions during the semester and/or about ending the relationship. As a supervisor, your self-disclosure is appropriate as it benefits the supervisee's learning about counseling and about relationships. If you have been supervised, you may also want to discuss that relationship during the last supervisory session.

Figure 7. Counselor evaluation of supervisor.

Supervisor _____ Counselor _____

	Strongly disagree		Somewhat agree		Strongly agree		
1. Provides me with useful feedback regarding counseling behavior.	1	2	3	4	5	6	7
2. Helps me feel at ease with the supervision process.	1	2	3	4	5	6	7
3. Makes supervision a constructive learning process.	1	2	3	4	5	6	7
4. Provides me with specific help in areas I need to work on.	1	2	3	4	5	6	7
5. Addresses issues relevant to my current concerns as a counselor.	1	2	3	4	5	6	7
6. Helps me focus on new alternative counseling strategies that I can use with my clients.	1	2	3	4	5	6	7
7. Helps me focus on how my counseling behavior influences the client.	1	2	3	4	5	6	7
8. Encourages me to try alternative counseling skills.	1	2	3	4	5	6	7
9. Structures supervision appropriately.	1	2	3	4	5	6	7
10. Adequately emphasizes the development of my strengths and capabilities.	1	2	3	4	5	6	7
11. Enables me to brainstormsolutions, responses, and techniques that would be helpful in future counseling situations.	1	2	3	4	5	6	7
12. Enables me to become actively involved in the supervision process.	1	2	3	4	5	6	7
13. Makes me feel accepted and respected as a person.	1	2	3	4	5	6	7
14. Deals appropriately with the affect in my counseling sessions.	1	2	3	4	5	6	7
15. Deals appropriately with the content in my counseling sessions.	1	2	3	4	5	6	7
16. Motivates me to assess my own counseling behavior.	1	2	3	4	5	6	7
17. Conveys competence.	1	2	3	4	5	6	7
18. Is helpful in critiquing report writing.	1	2	3	4	5	6	7
19. Helps me use tests constructively in counseling.	1	2	3	4	5	6	7
20. Appropriately addresses interpersonal dynamics between self and counselor.	1	2	3	4	5	6	7

		Strongly disagree			Somewhat agree			Strongly agree
21.	Can accept feedback from counselor.	1	2	3	4	5	6	7
22.	Helps reduce defensiveness in supervision.	1	2	3	4	5	6	7
23.	Enables me to express opinions, questions, and concerns about my counseling.	1	2	3	4	5	6	7
24.	Prepares me adequately for my next counseling session.	1	2	3	4	5	6	7
25.	Helps me clarify my counseling objectives.	1	2	3	4	5	6	7
26.	Provides me with the opportunity to adequately discuss the major difficulties I am facing with my clients.	1	2	3	4	5	6	7
27.	Encourages me to conceptualize in new ways regarding my clients.	1	2	3	4	5	6	7
28.	Motivates me and encourages me.	1	2	3	4	5	6	7
29.	Challenges me to accurately perceive the thoughts, feelings, and goals of my client and myself during counseling.	1	2	3	4	5	6	7
30.	Gives me the chance to discuss personal issues related to my counseling.	1	2	3	4	5	6	7
31.	Is flexible enough for me to be spontaneous and creative.	1	2	3	4	5	6	7
32.	Focuses on the implications and consequences of specific behaviors in my counseling approach.	1	2	3	4	5	6	7
33.	Provides suggestions for developing my counseling skills.	1	2	3	4	5	6	7
34.	Encourages me to use new and different techniques when appropriate.	1	2	3	4	5	6	7
35.	Helps me to define and achieve specific concrete goals for myself during the practicum experience.	1	2	3	4	5	6	7
36.	Gives me useful feedback.	1	2	3	4	5	6	7
37.	Helps me organize relevant case data in planning goals and strategies with my client.	1	2	3	4	5	6	7
38.	Helps me develop increased skill in critiquing and gaining insight from my counseling tapes.	1	2	3	4	5	6	7
39.	Allows and encourages me to evaluate myself.	1	2	3	4	5	6	7
40.	Explains the criteria for evaluation clearly and in behavioral terms.	1	2	3	4	5	6	7
41.	Applies criteria fairly in evaluating my counseling performance.	1	2	3	4	5	6	7

Additional comments:

This form was developed by Janine M. Bernard (1976; revised, 1981). Reprinted by permission.

Figure 8. Competencies of supervisors.

	Needs Development				Expertise

I. CONCEPTUAL SKILLS AND KNOWLEDGE
A. *Generic Skills*
THE SUPERVISOR IS ABLE TO DEMONSTRATE KNOWLEDEGE AND CONCEPTUAL UNDERSTANDING OF THE FOLLOWING:

1. the methodology of supervision, including	1	2	3	4	5
a) facilitative processes (consultation, counseling, education, or training and evaluation).	1	2	3	4	5
b) basic approaches (e.g., psychotherapeutic, behavioral, integrative, systems, developmental).	1	2	3	4	5
2. a definition or explanation of supervision	1	2	3	4	5
3. the variety of settings in which counselor supervisors work.	1	2	3	4	5
4. the counselor's roles and functions in particular work settings.	1	2	3	4	5
5. the developmental nature of supervision.	1	2	3	4	5
6. appropriate supervisory interventions, including	1	2	3	4	5
a) role-playing.	1	2	3	4	5
b) role-reversal.	1	2	3	4	5
c) live observation and live supervision.	1	2	3	4	5
d) reviewing audio and videotapes.	1	2	3	4	5
e) giving direct suggestions and advice.	1	2	3	4	5
f) leading groups of 2 or more supervisees.	1	2	3	4	5
g) providing didactic experiences.	1	2	3	4	5
h) microtraining.	1	2	3	4	5
i) IPR.	1	2	3	4	5
j) other_____	1	2	3	4	5
7. credentialing standards for counselors.	1	2	3	4	5
8. counselor ethical practices.	1	2	3	4	5
9. various counseling theories.	1	2	3	4	5
10. his/her own personal theory of counseling	1	2	3	4	5
11. his/her assumptions about human behavior.	1	2	3	4	5

	Needs Development			Expertise	

	Needs Development			Expertise	
12. models of supervision.	1	2	3	4	5
13. the meaning of accountability and the supervisor's responsibility in promoting this condition.	1	2	3	4	5
14. human growth and development.	1	2	3	4	5
15. motivation and needs theory.	1	2	3	4	5
16. learning theory.	1	2	3	4	5
17. resources and information to assist in addressing program goals and client needs.	1	2	3	4	5

B. *Supervision of Practicing Counselors*
THE SUPERVISOR IS ABLE TO DEMONSTRATE KNOWLEDGE AND CONCEPTUAL UNDERSTANDING OF THE FOLLOWING:

18. legal considerations affecting counselor practice	1	2	3	4	5
19. various intervention activities and strategies that would complement the counseling program goals.	1	2	3	4	5

C. *Supervision of Counselors-in-Training (covered in Generic Skills above)*

D. *Program Management/Supervision*
THE SUPERVISOR IS ABLE TO DEMONSTRATE KNOWLEDGE AND CONCEPTUAL UNDERSTANDING OF THE FOLLOWING:

20. his/her basic management theory.	1	2	3	4	5
21. various program development models.	1	2	3	4	5
22. decision-making theory.	1	2	3	4	5
23. organization development theory.	1	2	3	4	5
24. conflict resolution techniques.	1	2	3	4	5
25. leadership styles.	1	2	3	4	5
26. computerized information systems.	1	2	3	4	5
27. time-management techniques.	1	2	3	4	5

II. DIRECT INTERVENTION SKILLS

A. *Generic Skills*
THE SUPERVISOR IS ABLE TO DEMONSTRATE INTERVENTION TECHNIQUES IN THE FOLLOWING WAYS:

1. provide structure for supervision sessions, including	1	2	3	4	5
a) stating the purposes of supervision.	1	2	3	4	5

	Needs Development			Expertise	
b) clarifying the goals and direction of supervision.	1	2	3	4	5
c) clarifying his/her own role in supervision.	1	2	3	4	5
d) explaining the procedures to be followed in supervision.	1	2	3	4	5
2. identify the learning needs of the supervisee.	1	2	3	4	5
3. determine the extent to which the supervisee has developed and applied his/her own personal theory of counseling.	1	2	3	4	5
4. provide specific feedback about supervisee's.	1	2	3	4	5
a) conceptualization of client concerns.	1	2	3	4	5
b) process of counseling.	1	2	3	4	5
c) personalization of counseling.	1	2	3	4	5
d) performance of other related duties.	1	2	3	4	5
5. implement a variety of supervisory interventions (see Conceptual Skills & Knowledge).	1	2	3	4	5
6. negotiate mutual decisions regarding the needed direction of learning experiences for the supervisee.	1	2	3	4	5
7. use media aids for assisting with supervision.	1	2	3	4	5
8. develop evaluation procedures and instruments to determine program and supervisee goal attainment.	1	2	3	4	5
9. monitor the use of tests and test interpretations.	1	2	3	4	5
10. assist with the referral process, when appropriate.	1	2	3	4	5
11. facilitate and monitor research to determine the effectiveness of programs, services, and techniques.	1	2	3	4	5

B. *Program Management/Supervision*
THE SUPERVISOR IS ABLE TO DEMONSTRATE INTERVENTION TECHNIQUES IN THE FOLLOWING WAYS:

12. develop role descriptions for all staff positions.	1	2	3	4	5
13. conduct a needs assessment.	1	2	3	4	5
14. write goals and objectives.	1	2	3	4	5
15. monitor the progress of program activities.	1	2	3	4	5
16. monitor the progress of staff's responsibilities.	1	2	3	4	5
17. utilize decision-making techniques.	1	2	3	4	5

	Needs Development			Expertise	
18. apply problem-solving techniques.	1	2	3	4	5
19. conduct and coordinate staff development training.	1	2	3	4	5
20. implement management information systems.	1	2	3	4	5
21. employ group management strategies.	1	2	3	4	5
22. schedule tasks and develop time lines according to the needs of supervisees and the program.	1	2	3	4	5
23. maintain appropriate forms and records to assist with supervisory duties.	1	2	3	4	5
24. monitor supervisee report-writing andrecord-keeping skills.	1	2	3	4	5
25. diagnose organizational problems.	1	2	3	4	5
26. employ systematic observation techniques.	1	2	3	4	5
27. plan and administer a budget.	1	2	3	4	5
28. conduct follow-up studies and applied research.	1	2	3	4	5
29. establish consistent and quality hiring and affirmative action practices.	1	2	3	4	5
30. delegate responsibility.	1	2	3	4	5

III. HUMAN SKILLS

A. *Generic Skills*
THE SUPERVISOR IS ABLE TO APPLY THE FOLLOWING INTERACTION SKILLS IN A SUPERVISORY CAPACITY:

	Needs Development			Expertise	
1. deal with the supervisee from the perspective of	1	2	3	4	5
a) teacher.	1	2	3	4	5
b) counselor.	1	2	3	4	5
c) consultant.	1	2	3	4	5
d) evaluator.	1	2	3	4	5
2. describe his/her own pattern of dealing with interpersonal relationships.	1	2	3	4	5
3. integrate knowledge of supervision with own style of inter-personal relations.	1	2	3	4	5

	Needs Development			Expertise	
4. create facilitative conditions (empathy, concreteness, respect, congruence, genuineness, and immediacy).	1	2	3	4	5
5. establish a mutually trusting relationship with the supervisee.	1	2	3	4	5
6. establish a therapeutic relationship when appropriate.	1	2	3	4	5
7. identify supervisee's professional and personal strengths, as well as weaknesses.	1	2	3	4	5
8. clarify supervisee's personal needs (behavior mannerisms, personal crises, appearance, etc.), as well as professional needs that affect counseling.	1	2	3	4	5
9. elicit supervisee feelings during counseling or consultation sessions.	1	2	3	4	5
10. elicit supervisee perceptions of counseling dynamics.	1	2	3	4	5
11. use confrontation skills when identifying supervisee's inconsistencies.	1	2	3	4	5
12. elicit new alternatives from supervisee for identifying solutions, techniques, responses, etc.	1 4	5	2		3
13. demonstrate skill in the application of counseling techniques (both individual and group) that are appropriate for the work setting.	1	2	3	4	5
14. assist the supervisee in structuring his/her own self-supervision.	1	2	3	4	5
15. conduct self-evaluations as a means of modeling appropriate professional growth.	1	2	3	4	5
16. identify own strengths and weaknesses as a supervisor.	1	2	3	4	5
17. model appropriate behaviors expected of supervisees.	1	2	3	4	5
18. demonstrate and enforce ethical/professional standards.	1	2	3	4	5

B. *Traits and Qualities*
THE SUPERVISOR POSSESSES THE FOLLOWING TRAITS OR QUALITIES:

1. demonstrates a commitment to the role of supervisor.	1	2	3	4	5
2. is comfortable with the authority inherent in the role of supervisor.	1	2	3	4	5
3. has a sense of humor.	1	2	3	4	5
4. is encouraging, optimistic, and motivational.	1	2	3	4	5
5. expects supervisees to own the consequences of their actions.	1	2	3	4	5

	Needs Development			Expertise	
6. is sensitive to individual differences.	1	2	3	4	5
7. is sensitive to supervisee's needs.	1	2	3	4	5
8. is committed to updating his/her own counseling and supervisory skills.	1	2	3	4	5
9. recognizes that the ultimate goal of supervision is helping the client of the supervisee.	1	2	3	4	5
10. maintains open communication between supervisees and the supervisor.	1	2	3	4	5
11. monitors the "energy level" of supervisees to identify possible signs of counselor burnout in advance of possible crises.	1	2	3	4	5
12. recognizes own limits through eliciting self-evaluation and feedback from others.	1	2	3	4	5
13. enjoys and appreciates the role of supervisor.	1	2	3	4	5

This list of supervision competencies was adopted by the ACES Supervision Interest Network (C. E. VanZandt, Chair), at the AACD Convention, New York, April 2, 1985.

Epilogue

To the Instructor/Supervisor of the Beginning Supervisor

Although this *Handbook* was primarily written for the counseling supervisor, it was also designed for use by instructors of counseling supervision courses, supervisors of beginning supervisors, and trainers of in-service workshops for new field-site supervisors. The chapters in the *Handbook* are arranged to help guide supervisors through the sequence of experiences they will encounter in their first (and subsequent) supervision work. The sequence presented includes procedures (e.g., establishing a contract, assessing and evaluating the supervisee), roles of the supervisor, interventions, process issues (e.g., supervisee resistance), and ethical and legal concerns. Other chapters emphasize the importance of self-assessment and evaluation of supervision knowledge, skills, and performance.

The same sequence and issues outlined for the supervisor's work with a student counselor can be adapted to the instructor/supervisor's work with the beginning supervisor. For example, the instructor/supervisor will also want to do the following:

1. Conduct an initial assessment of the beginning supervisor's performance and conceptual skills in the roles of the supervisor (e.g., teacher, counselor, consultant), developmental level, and learning style.

2. Establish learning goals and agree to a contract for procedures and expectations for the course and/or supervised practicum (these would include instructor-determined competencies for "passing" and course assignments, in addition to more individual student-determined needs and goals).

3. Choose appropriate techniques and interventions based on the assessment and goals.

4. Evaluate the beginning supervisor.

71

5. Deal with process issues (e.g., resistance, instructor/supervisor— beginning supervisor relationship, parallel processes).

6. Consider ethical and legal issues (e.g., the instructor/supervisor's responsibilities to and for the beginning supervisor, the supervisee, and the client).

Many of the assessment procedures, interventions, and evaluation instruments suggested in the *Handbook* are appropriate for instructors/supervisors to use with beginning supervisors, in addition to teaching them to the beginning supervisor. Instructors/supervisors will also want to solicit feedback on their course and/or supervision of beginning supervisors.

Novice Supervisors

The novice supervisor and the novice counselor have many similarities as each begins the process of taking on a new role and identity. For this reason, we might speculate that the beginning supervisor would experience developmental concerns and follow developmental stages parallel to those described in developmental models of counseling supervision (Borders, 1983a).

Several models of supervisor development briefly outline sequences and issues somewhat similar to those in models of counselor development. These models include psychodynamic (Alonso, 1983), cognitive-developmental (McPherson, Amerikaner, & Edwards, 1985), career developmental (Lazarus, 1986) and more general (Hess, 1986) descriptions of stages of development. Generally, novice supervisors in these models are described as apprehensive, somewhat defensive, and in a state of "identity diffusion" (Alonso, 1983) as they try to take on a new role, create a self-image as a supervisor, and project themselves as an expert. Because of this self-focus, they may be unable to recognize the individual differences of their supervisees or establish a good working relationship with the supervisee. Like the counselors described by Loganbill et al. (1982) and Stoltenberg (1981), they struggle with issues of competency, autonomy, and identity.

Novice supervisors who attended a presentation at the 1985 AACD Convention (McPherson et al., 1985) exemplified these concerns. One doctoral student facing her first experience as a supervisor said she felt overwhelmed by a sense of responsibility for the counselor and client, and concern for the counselor who would be her "guinea pig." Others wondered aloud about possible challenges to their authority and the "difficulty of handling power." In addition, the results of a survey of inexperienced (less than two years) supervisors indicated the most frequently reported difficulties were dealing with supervisee resistance and feelings of not knowing what was happening in the case nor how to intervene in the case (McColley & Baker, 1982).

The instructor/supervisor, then, can adapt developmental models of counselor supervision to assess the novice supervisor's developmental level and create appropriate learning environments. Interventions would probably be structured and include direct teaching, modeling, role playing, audiotape and videotape reviewing. Beginning supervisors would also need support and encouragement to conceptualize the supervisees' needs and skills and to try their own approaches to supervision.

To deal with their issues around authority and evaluation, some beginning supervisors may be more authoritative and critical of their supervisees in their efforts to maintain control and to be identified with those in power (Alonso, 1983; McPherson et al., 1985). Others may instead overidentify with their supervisees as a result of memories of supervision experiences in which they felt like the victims of the power structure (Alonso, 1983), or become overinvolved because of their intensity in this first experience (Rosenblatt & Mayer, 1975). These are tendencies, then, the instructor/supervisor may recognize in beginning supervisors.

Results of the few published studies of beginning supervisors indicate they may be more experiential than instructive (Marikis, Russell, & Dell, 1985; Smith, 1976) and less willing to reveal themselves (Marikis et al., 1985) than more experienced supervisors. They also tend to give little feedback and use few confrontive statements with supervisees (Diehl, 1982, and cited in Cormier & Bernard, 1982). Instructors/supervisors, then, may need to instruct, model, and encourage the use of these behaviors when they are appropriate. Attention to these behaviors may be especially important if the novice is supervising a beginning counselor who needs the instruction and specific feedback the novice is hesitant to give.

Supervision Instruction

A few models for teaching supervision have been published that could serve as guides for the instructor/supervisor. Several models are also illustrated on videotapes to aid instruction.

Richardson and Bradley (1984), for example, have adapted the microtraining training approach for teaching counseling supervision skills to counselor educators and agency supervisors. Their microsupervision model has three stages: 1) assessment of skill proficiencies and deficits, ranking of deficits in a hierarchy; 2) videotaped modeling of ineffective and effective examples of each skill, role-playing, and discussion of the cognitive and affective components involved in that skill; and 3) transfer of skill, based on supervisor and self-evaluation of performance. When proficiency has been reached, the procedure is repeated for the next skill. The authors believe the microsupervision model allows for individualized instruction of supervision skills.

Loganbill and her associates (Loganbill & Hardy, 1983; Loganbill et al., 1982) have outlined a program with three sequential training components: (a) theoretical content (e.g., history, theoretical orientations, process, research, cultural and sex-role issues, ethical and legal aspects); (b) simulated experience (e.g., role taking and role-playing); and (c) actual "in vivo" practice (e.g., supervised supervision of a student counselor).

Beginning supervisors integrate the conceptual and experiential components with their personal qualities to clarify a personal style of supervision and a self-identity as a supervisor.

Bernard (1979) has developed a discrimination model and training package (Bernard, 1981) for the training of counseling supervisors that has been used as a pre-practicum course for doctoral students and in-service training for field-site supervisors. The discrimination model identifies three functions of supervision as developing counselor competency in (a) process skills (e.g., overt, observable behaviors such as beginning and ending a session, use of reflections, probes, interpretations), (b) conceptualization skills (e.g., case analysis to identify themes and patterns and to choose appropriate interventions), and (c) personalization skills (e.g., lack of defensiveness in response to client challenges, comfort with authority in counseling relationship). A supervisor can focus on each of these areas in any of the three roles of teacher, counselor, or consultant.

Objectives of the discrimination model include helping a supervisor make a deliberate choice of role and skill areas focus based on the needs of the counselor, and providing a "common language" for analyzing participants' baseline supervision behaviors and discussing the interventions introduced in later training sessions. During the training, participants rehearse and role-play interventions that fit into each role, including microtraining (teacher) and Interpersonal Process Recall (consultant and counselor). The training also includes sessions that allow participants to practice giving evaluative feedback to the supervisee and dealing with ethical situations such as emergency referrals and unethical counselor behavior.

Spice and Spice (1976) describe a triadic method for training supervisors. Working in groups of three, beginning supervisors take turns functioning in three different roles: beginning supervisor, commentator, and facilitator. The beginning supervisor presents samples (e.g., audiotape, videotape, case report) of an actual supervision session, the commentator previews the sample and then shares observations and encourages dialogue about the session, and the facilitator comments on the present, here-and-now dialogue between the beginning supervisor and the commentator. Four processes are taught in the triadic model: (a) presentation of supervision work, (b) art of critical commentary, (c) engagement of meaningful self-dialogue, and (d) deepening of the here-and-now process. A faculty member meets with the triad to serve as a role model and provide training in the skills of critical commentary and here-and-now observations.

In Davis and Arvey's (1978) dual supervision model, the same supervisee is assigned to a beginning supervisor and a faculty member. The two supervisors meet on alternate weeks with the supervisee for an individual session. The two supervisors also meet weekly to review audiotapes of the beginning supervisor's sessions, discuss the supervisee's progress, and brainstorm supervision interventions.

A few audiovisual aids are also available. Hart (1982) has developed a series of videotapes that depict his three models of supervision: skill development, personal growth, and integration. Each model varies in the functional relationship of the supervisor-supervisee (e.g., teacher-student, therapist-client, collaborative), the hierarchial distance in that relationship, and focus of the supervision session (e.g., counseling skills, counselor self-awareness, integration of skills and personal awareness). Hart has produced additional videotapes that illustrate impasses in the supervisor-supervisee relationship and critical moments during supervision.

Goodyear (1982) has also developed videotapes that may be used in training counseling supervisors. In his series, supervision sessions are conducted by major counseling theorists, including Polster (Gestalt), Rogers (client-centered), Kagan (IPR), Ekstein (psychoanalytic), and Ellis (RET).

Summary

The content and sequential procedure for supervising counselors presented in this *Handbook* can be adapted for supervising supervisors. A developmental perspective of supervisors suggests appropriate interventions for the novice supervisor, and several instructional models offer guidelines and audiovisual aids for training supervisors.

It is hoped the increased attention to training supervisors, including the publication of this *Handbook,* will lead to more effective supervision by knowledgeable and skilled supervisors. Competent supervision is more likely to result in competent counseling and, in turn, more fully-functioning clients.

References

Abramowitz, S. I., & Abramowitz, C. V. (1976). Sex-role dynamics in psychotherapy supervision. *American Journal of Psychotherapy, 30,* 583-592.

Akamatsu, T. J. (1980). The use of role-play and simulation techniques in the training of psychotherapy. In A. K. Hess (Ed.), *Psychotherapy supervision: Theory, research and practice* (pp. 209-225). New York: Wiley.

Aldrich, L., & Hess, A. K. (1983, March). Parallel process: Its prevalence, content and resolution in counseling and psychotherapy supervision. Paper presented at the meeting of the Southeastern Psychological Association, Atlanta, GA.

Allen, G. J., Szollos, S. J., & Williams, B. E. (1986). Doctoral students' comparative evaluations of best and worst psychotherapy supervision. *Professional Psychology, 17,* 91-99.

Alonso, A. (1983). A developmental theory of psychodynamic supervision. *The Clinical Supervisor, 1*(3), 23-36.

Arbuckle, D. G. (1963). The learning of counseling: Process not product. *Journal of Counseling Psychology, 10,* 165-166.

Ashby, J. D., Ford, D. H., Guerney, B. G., & Guerney, L. F. (1957). Effects on clients of a reflective and leading type of psychotherapy. *Psychological Monographs, 71,* 1-32.

Atkinson, D. R., & Wampold, B. E. (1982). A comparison of the Counselor Rating Form and Counselor Effectiveness Rating Scale. *Counselor Education and Supervision, 22,* 25-36.

Atkinson, D. R., & Zimmer, J. M. (1977). The counselor trainee portfolio. *Counselor Education and Supervision, 16,* 257-262.

Barak, A., & LaCrosse, M. B. (1975). Multidimensional perception of counselor behavior. *Journal of Counseling Psychology, 22,* 471-476.

Barrett-Lennard, G. T. (1962). Dimensions of therapist response as causal factors in therapeutic change. *Psychological Monographs, 76* (43, Whole No. 562).

Bartlett, W. E. (1983). A multidimensional framework for the analysis of supervision of counseling. *The Counseling Psychologist, 11*(1), 9-17.

Bartlett, W. E., Goodyear, R. K., & Bradley, F. O. (Eds.). (1983). Supervision in counseling II [Special issue]. *The Counseling Psychologist, 11*(1).

Baum, D., & Lane, J. (1976). An application of "bug-in-the-ear" communication for training psychometrists. *Counselor Education and Supervision, 15,* 309-310.

Bauman, W. F. (1972). Games counselor trainees play: Dealing with trainee resistance. *Counselor Education and Supervision, 11,* 251-256.

Bernard, J. M. (1979). Supervisory training: A discrimination model. *Counselor Education and Supervision, 19,* 60-68.

Bernard, J. M. (1981). Inservice training for clinical supervisors. *Professional Psychology, 12,* 740-748.

Bernard, J. M. (1982). A training laboratory in clinical supervision. Unpublished manuscript.

Bernier, J. E. (1980). Training and supervising counselors: Lessons learned from deliberate psychological education. *Personnel and Guidance Journal, 59,* 15-20.

Bernstein, B. L., Hofmann, B., & Wade, P. (1986). Counselor self-supervision: Beyond traditional approaches to practicum supervision. *Michigan Journal of Counseling and Development, 17*(2), 13-17.

Bernstein, B. L., & Lecomte, C. (1979). Self-critique technique training in a competency-based practicum. *Counselor Education and Supervision, 19,* 69-76.

Birchler, G. (1975). Live supervision and instant feedback in marriage and family therapy. *Journal of Marriage and Family Counseling, 1,* 331-342.

Blocher, D. H. (1983). Toward a cognitive developmental approach to counseling supervision. *The Counseling Psychologist, 11*(1), 27-34.

Blumberg, A. (1970). A system for analyzing supervisor-teacher interaction. In A. Simon & G. Boyer (Eds.), *Mirrors for behavior* (Vol. 3). Philadelphia: Research for Better Schools.

Borders, L. D. (1983a, October). Supervising the novice supervisor. Presentation at the meeting of the Southern Association for Counselor Education and Supervision, Mobile, AL.

Borders, L. D. (1983b, November). The novice supervisor. Presentation at the meeting of the Florida Personnel and Guidance Association, Daytona Beach, FL.

Borders, L. D. (1986). Facilitating supervisee growth: Implications of developmental models of counseling supervision. *Michigan Journal of Counseling and Development, 17*(2), 7-12.

Borders, L. D., Fong, M. L., & Neimeyer, G. J. (1986). Counseling students' level of ego development and perceptions of clients. *Counselor Education and Supervision, 26,* 36-49.

Bordin, E. S. (1983). A working alliance based model of supervision. *The Counseling Psychologist, 11*(1), 35-42.

Boyd, J. (1978). *Counselor supervision: Approaches, preparation, practices.* Muncie, IN: Accelerated Development.

Boylston, W., & Tuma, J. (1972). Training mental health professionals through the use of a "bug in the ear." *American Journal of Psychiatry, 129,* 124-127.

Brodsky, A. M. (1980). Sex role issues in the supervision of therapy. In A. K. Hess (Ed.), *Psychotherapy supervision: Theory, research and practice* (pp. 509-522). New York: Wiley.

Butcher, E., & Scofield, M. E. (1984). Use of a standardized simulation and process tracing for studying clinical problem-solving competence. *Counselor Education and Supervision, 24,* 70-84.

Butcher, E., Scofield, M. E., & Baker, S. B. (1984). Validation of a simulation for the assessment of competence in mental health counselors. *AMHCA Journal, 6,* 162-172.

Butcher, E., Scofield, M. E., & Baker, S. B. (1985). Clinical judgment in planning mental health treatment: An empirical investigation. *AMHCA Journal, 7,* 116-126.

Clairborn, C. D., & Dixon, D. N. (1982). The acquisition of conceptual skills: An exploratory study. *Counselor Education and Supervision, 21,* 274-281.

Cohen, R. J. (1979). *Malpractice: A guide for mental health professionals.* New York: Free Press.

Conver, B. J. (1944). Studies in phonographic recordings of verbal material. The completeness and accuracy of counseling interview reports. *Journal of General Psychology, 30,* 181-203.

Coppersmith, E. (1980). Expanding uses of the telephone in family therapy. *Family Process, 19,* 411-417.

Corey, G., Corey, M. S., & Callanan, P. (1984). *Issues and ethics in the helping professions* (2nd ed.). Monterey, CA: Brooks/Cole.

Cormier, L. S., & Bernard, J. M. (1982). Ethical and legal responsibilities of clinical supervision. *Personnel and Guidance Journal, 60,* 486-491.

Corrigan, J. D., & Schmidt, L. D. (1983). Development and validation of revisions in the Counselor Rating Form. *Journal of Counseling Psychology, 30,* 64-75.

Cross, D. G., & Brown, D. (1983). Counselor supervision as a function of trainee experience: Analysis of specific behaviors. *Counselor Education and Supervision, 22,* 333-341.

Curtis, M. J., & Yager, G. G. (1981). A systems model for the supervision of school psychological services. *School Psychology Review, 10,* 425-433.

Davis, K. L., & Arvey, H. H. (1978). Dual supervision: A model for counseling and supervision. *Counselor Education and Supervision, 17,* 293-299.

Delaney, D. J. (1972). A behavioral model for the practicum supervision of counselor candidates. *Counselor Education and Supervision, 12,* 46-50.

Diehl, C. S. (1982). A naturalistic observation of supervision skill responses across time (Doctoral dissertation, West Virginia University, 1981). *Dissertation Abstracts International, 42,* 4298A. (University Microfilms No. DA8207505)

Dimick, K. M., & Krause, F. H. (1980). *Practicum manual for counseling and psychotherapy.* Muncie, IN: Accelerated Development.

Dodds, J. B. (1986). Supervision of psychology trainees in field placements. *Professional Psychology, 17,* 296-300.

Dodge, J. (1982). Reducing supervisee anxiety: A cognitive-behavioral approach. *Counselor Education and Supervision, 22,* 55-60.

Doehrman, M. J. (1976). Parallel processes in supervision and psychotherapy. *Bulletin of the Menninger Clinic, 40,* 1-104.

Dustin, R. E., Engen, H. B., & Shymansky, J. A. (1982). The ICB: A tool for counselor supervision. *Counselor Education and Supervision, 22,* 70-74.

Dyer, W. W., & Vriend, J. (1977). *Counseling techniques that work.* New York: Funk & Wagnalls.

Egan G. (1986). *The skilled helper* (3rd ed.). Monterey, CA: Brooks/Cole.

Ekstein, R., & Wallerstein, R. S. (1958). *The teaching and learning of psychotherapy.* New York: Basic Books.

Ekstein, R., & Wallerstein, R. S. (1972). *The teaching and learning of psychotherapy* (2nd ed.). New York: International Universities Press.

Fink, R., Allen, R., & Barak, A. (1986). Teaching and supervising career assessment interns. *Michigan Journal of Counseling and Development, 17*(2), 25-28.

Forsyth, D. R., & Ivey, A. E. (1980). Microtraining: An approach to differential supervision. In A. K. Hess (Ed.), *Psychotherapy supervision: Theory, research and practice* (pp. 242-261). New York: Wiley.

Fraleigh, P. W., & Buchheimer, A. (1969). The use of peer groups in practicum supervision. *Counselor Education and Supervision, 8,* 284-288.

Friedlander, M. L., & Ward, L. G. (1984). Development and validation of the Supervisory Styles Inventory. *Journal of Counseling Psychology, 31,* 541-557.

Fuller, F., & Hill, C. E. (1985). Counselor and helpee perceptions of counselor intentions in relation to outcome in a single counseling session. *Journal of Counseling Psychology, 32,* 329-338.

Fuqua, D. R., Johnson, A. W., Anderson, M. W., & Newman, J. L. (1984). Cognitive methods in counselor training. *Counselor Education and Supervision, 24,* 85-95.

Gaoni, B., & Neumann, M. (1974). Supervision from the point of view of the supervisee. *American Journal of Psychotherapy, 23,* 108-114.

Gardner, L. H. (1980). Racial, ethnic, and social class considerations in psychotherapy supervision. In A. K. Hess (Ed.), *Psychotherapy supervision: Theory, research and practice* (pp. 474-508). New York: Wiley.

Gazda, G. M., Asbury, F. R., Balzer, F. J., Childers, W. C., & Walters, R. P. (1984). *Human relations development* (3rd ed.). Boston: Allyn & Bacon.

Goodyear, R. K. (Producer). (1982). Psychotherapy supervision by major theorists [Videotape series]. Manhattan: Instructional Media Center, Kansas State University.

Goodyear, R. K. (1985, April). Reducing trainee anxiety through videotaped role induction. Presentation at the annual meeting of the American Association for Counseling and Development, New York.

Goodyear, R. K., Abadie, P. D., & Efros, F. (1984). Supervisory theory into practice: Differential perception of supervision by Ekstein, Ellis, Polster, and Rogers. *Journal of Counseling Psychology, 31*, 228-237.

Goodyear, R. K., & Bradley, F. O. (1983). Theories of counselor supervision: Points of convergence and divergence. *The Counseling Psychologist, 11*(1), 59-67.

Goodyear, R. K., Bradley, F. O., & Bartlett, W. E. (1983). An introduction to theories of counselor supervision. *The Counseling Psychologist, 11*(1), 19-20.

Goodyear, R. K., & Robyak, J. E. (1982). Supervisors' theory and experience in supervisory focus. *Psychological Reports, 51*, 978.

Grater, H. A. (1985). Stages in psychotherapy supervision: From therapy skills to skilled therapist. *Professional Psychology, 16*, 605-610.

Greenberg, L. (1980). Training counsellors in Gestalt methods. *Canadian Counsellor, 15*, 174-180.

Gustin, J. C. (1958). Supervision in psychotherapy. *Psychoanalysis and Psychiatric Review, 45*(3), 63-72.

Gutheil, T. G. (1977). Ideology as resistance: A supervisory challenge. *Psychiatric Quarterly, 49*, 88-96.

Guttman, M. A. J. (1973). Reduction of the defensive behavior of counselor trainees during counseling supervision. *Counselor Education and Supervision, 12*, 294-299.

Gysbers, N. G., & Johnston, J. A. (1965). Expectations of a practicum supervisor's role. *Counselor Education and Supervision, 4*, 68-74.

Hackney, H. (1976). Practicum manual. Unpublished manuscript, Purdue University, West Lafayette, IN.

Hamatz, M. G. (1975). Two-channel recording in the supervision of psychotherapy. *Professional Psychology, 6*, 478-480.

Hansen, J. C., Pound, R., & Petro, C. (1976). Review of research on practicum supervision. *Counselor Education and Supervision, 16*, 107-116.

Hansen, J. C., Robins, T. H., & Grimes, J. (1982). Review of research on practicum supervision. *Counselor Education and Supervision, 22*, 15-24.

Hart, G. M. (1982). *The process of clinical supervision.* Baltimore: University Park Press.

Hart, G. M., & Falvey, E. (1986). Field supervision of counselor trainees: A survey of the North Atlantic Region. Unpublished manuscript.

Hawthorne, L. (1975). Games supervisors play. *Social Work, 20*, 179-183.

Heath, A. W., & Storm, C. L. (1983). Answering the call: A manual for beginning supervisors. *The Family Therapy Networker, 7*(2), 36-37, 66.

Heppner, P. P., & Handley, P. G. (1981). A study of the interpersonal influence process in supervision. *Journal of Counseling Psychology, 28*, 437-444.

Heppner, P. P., & Roehlke, H. J. (1984). Differences among supervisees at different levels of training: Implications for a developmental model of supervision. *Journal of Counseling Psychology, 31,* 76-90.

Hess, A. K. (Ed.). (1980). *Psychotherapy supervision: Theory, research and practice.* New York: Wiley.

Hess, A. K. (1986). Growth in supervision: Stages of supervisee and supervisor development. *The Clinical Supervisor, 4*(1-2), 51-67.

Hess, A. K., & Hess, K. A. (1983). Psychotherapy supervision: A survey of internship training practices. *Professional Psychology, 14,* 504-513.

Hill, C. E. (1978). Development of a counselor verbal response category system. *Journal of Counseling Psychology, 25,* 461-468.

Hill, C. E., Charles, D., & Reed, K. G. (1981). A longitudinal analysis of changes in counseling skills during doctoral training in counseling psychology. *Journal of Counseling Psychology, 28,* 428-436.

Hill, C. E., & O'Grady, K. E. (1985). List of therapist intentions illustrated in a case study and with therapists of varying theoretical orientations. *Journal of Counseling Psychology, 32,* 3-22.

Hogan, R. A. (1964). Issues and approaches in supervision. *Psychotherapy: Theory, research and practice, 1,* 139-141.

Holahan, W., & Galassi, J. P. (1986). Toward accountability in supervision: A single-case illustration. *Counselor Education and Supervision, 25,* 166-174.

Holloway, E. L. (1982). Characteristics of the field practicum: A national survey. *Counselor Education and Supervision, 22,* 75-80.

Holloway, E. L. (1984). Outcome evaluation in supervision research. *The Counseling Psychologist, 12*(4), 167-174.

Holloway, E. L., & Hosford, R. E. (1983). Towards developing a prescriptive technology of counselor supervision. *The Counseling Psychologist, 11*(1), 73-77.

Holloway, E. L., & Johnston, R. (1985). Group supervision: Widely practiced but poorly understood. *Counselor Education and Supervision, 24,* 332-340.

Holloway, E. L., & Wampold, B. E. (1983). Patterns of verbal behavior and judgments of satisfaction in the supervision interview. *Journal of Counseling Psychology, 30,* 227-234.

Holloway, E. L., & Wolleat, P. L. (1980). Relationship of counselor conceptual level to clinical hypothesis formation. *Journal of Counseling Psychology, 27,* 539-545.

Hora, T. (1957). Contributions to the phenomenology of the supervisory process. *American Journal of Psychotherapy, 11,* 769-773.

Hosford, R. E., & Barmann, B. (1983). A social learning approach to counselor supervision. *The Counseling Psychologist, 11*(1), 51-58.

Hulse, D., & Jennings, M. L. (1984). Toward comprehensive case conceptualizations in counseling: A visual integrative technique. *Professional Psychology, 15,* 251-259.

Hutt, C. H., Scott, J., & King, M. (1983). A phenomenological study of supervisees' positive and negative experiences in supervision. *Psychotherapy: Theory, Research and Practice, 20,* 118-123.

Ivey, A. E. (1971). *Microcounseling: Innovations in interviewer training.* Springfield, IL: Thomas.

Ivey, A. E. (1980). *Counseling and psychotherapy: Skills, theories, and practice.* Englewood Cliffs, NJ: Prentice-Hall.

Ivey, A. E., & Authier, J. (1978). *Microcounseling: Innovations in interviewing, counseling, psychotherapy, and psychoeducation* (2nd ed.). Springfield, IL: Thomas.

Johnston, J. A., & Gysbers, N. C. (1967). Essential characteristics of a supervisory relationship in counseling practicum. *Counselor Education and Supervision, 6,* 335-340.

Kadushin, A. (1968). Games people play in supervision. *Social Work, 13,* 23-32.

Kagan, N. (1975). *Interpersonal process recall: A method of influencing human interaction.* East Lansing, MI: Michigan State University.

Kagan, N. (1980). Influencing human interaction—Eighteen years with IPR. In A. K. Hess (Ed.), *Psychotherapy supervision: Theory, research and practice* (pp. 262-283). New York: Wiley.

Kagan, N., & Krathwohl, D. R. (1967). *Studies in human interaction: Interpersonal process recall stimulated by videotape.* East Lansing, MI: Michigan State University.

Kagan, N., Krathwohl, D. R., & Farquhar, W. W. (1965). IPR - *Interpersonal process recall: Stimulated recall by videotape.* East Lansing, MI: Michigan State University.

Kagan, N., Krathwohl, D. R., & Miller, R. (1963). Stimulated recall in therapy using videotape—a case study. *Journal of Counseling Psychology, 10,* 237-243.

Kaplan, D. M. (1983). Current trends in practicum supervision research. *Counselor Education and Supervision, 22,* 215-226.

Kelly, F. D. (1976). The counseling jury: A step toward accountability. *Counselor Education and Supervision, 15,* 228-232.

Kempster, S., & Savitsky, E. (1967). Training family therapists through live supervision. In N. Ackerman (Ed.), *Expanding theory and practice in family therapy* (pp. 125-134). New York: Family Service Association.

Kurpius, D. J., Benjamin, D., & Morran, D. K. (1985). Effects of teaching a cognitive strategy on counselor trainee internal dialogue and clinical hypothesis formulation. *Journal of Counseling Psychology, 32,* 263-271.

Lambert, M. J. (1980). Research and the supervisory process. In A. K. Hess (Ed.), *Psychotherapy supervision: Theory, research and practice* (pp. 423-450). New York: Wiley.

Langs, R. J. (1980). Supervision in the bipolar field. In A. K. Hess (Ed.), *Psychotherapy supervision: Theory, research and practice* (pp. 103-125). New York: Wiley.

Lanning, W. (1986). Development of the Supervisor Emphasis Rating Form. *Counselor Education and Supervision, 25,* 191-196.

Lazarus, A. A. (1981). *The practice of multimodal therapy.* New York: McGraw-Hill.

Lazarus, S. (1986, August). Development of supervisors: A conceptual model. In J. P. Galassi (Chair), *Unresolved issues in counseling supervision.* Symposium conducted at the meeting of the American Psychological Association, Washington, DC.

Leddick, G. R., & Bernard, J. M. (1980). The history of supervision: A critical review. *Counselor Education and Supervision, 19,* 186-196.

Liddle, B. J. (1986, August). Resistance in supervision: A response to perceived threat. In J. P. Galassi (Chair), *Unresolved issues in counseling supervision.* Symposium conducted at the meeting of the American Psychological Association, Washington, DC.

Liddle, H., & Halpin, R. (1978). Family therapy training and supervision literature: A comparative review. *Journal of Marriage and Family Counseling, 4,* 77-98.

Linden, J. D., Stone, S. C., & Shertzer, B. (1965). Development and evaluation of an inventory for rating counseling. *Personnel and Guidance Journal, 44,* 267-276.

Linehan, M. M. (1980). Supervision of behavior therapy. In A. K. Hess (Ed.), *Psychotherapy supervision: Theory, research and practice* (pp. 148-180). New York: Wiley.

Littrell, J. M., Lee-Borden, N., & Lorenz, J. (1979). A developmental framework for counseling supervision. *Counselor Education and Supervision, 19,* 129-136.

Loganbill, C., & Hardy, E. (1983). Developing training programs for clinical supervisors. *The Clinical Supervisor, 1*(3), 15-21.

Loganbill, C., Hardy, E., & Delworth, U. (1982). Supervision: A conceptual model. *The Counseling Psychologist, 10*(1), 3-42.

Loganbill, C., & Stoltenberg, C. (1983). The case conceptualization format: A training device for practicum. *Counselor Education and Supervision, 22,* 235-241.

Mabe, A. R., & Rollin, S. A. (1986). The role of a code of ethical standards in counseling. *Journal of Counseling and Development, 64,* 294-297.

Marikis, D. A., Russell, R. K., & Dell, D. M. (1985). Effects of supervisor experience level on planning and in-session supervisor verbal behavior. *Journal of Counseling Psychology, 32,* 410-416.

Marshall, W. R., & Confer, W. N. (1980). Psychotherapy supervision: Supervisees' perspective. In A. K. Hess (Ed.), *Psychotherapy supervision: Theory, research and practice* (pp. 92-100). New York: Wiley.

Martin, J. S., Goodyear, R. K., & Newton, F. B. (1986, August). Clinical supervision: An intensive case study. In M. L. Friedlander (Chair), *Innovative perspectives on the supervisory process.* Symposium conducted at the meeting of the American Psychological Association, Washington, DC.

Martin, J., Hiebert, B. A., & Marx, R. W. (1981). Instructional supervision in counselor training. *Counselor Education and Supervision, 20,* 193-202.

Matarazzo, R. G. (1978). Research on the teaching and learning of psychotherapeutic skills. In S. L. Garfield & A. E. Bergin (Eds.), *Handbook of psychotherapy and behavior change: An empirical analysis* (2nd ed.) (pp. 941-966). New York: Wiley.

83

McClure, W. J., & Vriend, J. (1976). Training counsellors using absentee-cueing system. *Canadian Counsellor, 10,* 120-126.

McColley, S. H., & Baker, E. L. (1982). Training activities and styles of beginning supervisors: A survey. *Professional Psychology, 13,* 283-292.

McNeill, B. W., Stoltenberg, C. D., & Pierce, R. A. (1985). Supervisees' perceptions of their development: A test of the counselor complexity model. *Journal of Counseling Psychology, 32,* 630-633.

McPherson, R. H., Amerikaner, M. J., & Edwards, T. (1985, April). Supervisor development: A sequential hierarchy. Presentation at the meeting of the American Association for Counseling and Development, New York, NY.

Miars, R. D., Tracey, T. J., Ray, P. B., Cornfeld, J. L., O'Farrell, M., & Gelso, C. J. (1983). Variation in supervision process across trainee experience levels. *Journal of Counseling Psychology, 30,* 403-412.

Moldawsky, S. (1980). Psychoanalytic psychotherapy supervision. In A. K. Hess (Ed.), *Psychotherapy supervision: Theory, research and practice* (pp. 126-135). New York: Wiley.

Moses, H. A., & Hardin, J. T. (1978). A relationship approach to counselor supervision in agency settings. In J. D. Boyd (Ed.), *Counselor supervision: Approaches, preparation, practices* (pp. 437-480). Muncie, IN: Accelerated Development.

Moskowitz, S. A. (1981). A developmental model for the supervision of psychotherapy: The effect of level of experience on trainees' views of ideal supervision (Doctoral dissertation, Loyola University, 1981). *Dissertation Abstracts International, 42,* 1184B-1185B. (University Microfilms No. 8119985)

Moskowitz, S. A., & Rupert, P. A. (1983). Conflict resolution within the supervisory relationship. *Professional Psychology, 14,* 632-641.

Mueller, W. J., & Kell, B. L. (1972). *Coping with conflict: Supervising counselors and psychotherapists.* Englewood Cliffs, NJ: Prentice-Hall.

Myrick, R. D., & Kelly, F. D. (1971). A scale for evaluating practicum students in counseling and supervision. *Counselor Education and Supervision, 10,* 330-336.

Nash, V. C. (1975). The clinical supervision of psychotherapy (Doctoral dissertation, Yale University, 1975). *Dissertation Abstracts International, 36,* 2480B-2481B. (University Microfilms No. 75-24,581)

Nelson, G. L. (1978). Psychotherapy supervision from the trainee's point of view: A survey of preferences. *Professional Psychology, 9,* 539-550.

Newman, A. S. (1981). Ethical issues in the supervision of psychotherapy. *Professional Psychology, 12,* 690-695.

O'Malley, S. S., Suh, C. S., & Strupp, H. H. (1983). The Vanderbilt Psychotherapy Process Scale: A report on the scale development and a process-outcome study. *Journal of Consulting and Clinical Psychology, 51,* 581-586.

Patterson, C. H. (1983). A client-centered approach to supervision. *The Counseling Psychologist, 11*(1), 21-25.

Ponterotto, J. G., & Furlong, M. J. (1985). Evaluating counselor effectiveness: A critical review of rating scale instruments. *Journal of Counseling Psychology, 32,* 597-616.

Ponterotto, J. G., & Zander, T. A. (1984). A multimodal approach to counselor supervision. *Counselor Education and Supervision, 24,* 40-50.

Porter, E. J., Jr. (1950). *An introduction to therapeutic counseling.* Boston: Houghton-Mifflin.

Presser, N. R., & Pfost, K. S. (1985). A format for individual psychotherapy session notes. *Professional Psychology, 16,* 11-16.

Rabinowitz, F. E., Heppner, P. P., & Roehlke, H. J. (1986). Descriptive study of process and outcome variables of supervision over time. *Journal of Counseling Psychology, 33,* 292-300.

Reising, G. N., & Daniels, M. H. (1983). A study of Hogan's model of counselor development and supervision. *Journal of Counseling Psychology, 30,* 235-244.

Rice, L. N. (1980). A client-centered approach to the supervision of psychotherapy. In A. K. Hess (Ed.), *Psychotherapy supervision: Theory, research and practice* (pp. 136-147). New York: Wiley.

Richardson, B. K., & Bradley, L. J. (1984). Microsupervision: A skill development model for training clinical supervisors. *The Clinical Supervisor, 2*(3), 43-54.

Rioch, M. J., Coulter, W. R., & Weinberger, D. M. (1976). *Dialogues for therapists.* San Francisco, CA: Jossey-Bass.

Robiner, W. N. (1982). Role diffusion in the supervisory relationship. *Professional Psychology, 13,* 258-267.

Rosenblatt, A., & Mayer, J. E. (1975). Objectionable supervisory styles: Students' views. *Social Work, 20,* 184-189.

Rozsnafszky, J. (1979). Beyond schools of psychotherapy: Integrity and maturity in therapy and supervision. *Psychotherapy: Theory, Research and Practice, 16*(2), 190-198.

Rubinstein, K. E. (1980). Identification process in psychotherapy supervision: The effect of sex of student and supervisor (Doctoral dissertation, University of Massachusetts, 1979). *Dissertation Abstracts International, 40,* 3964B. (University Microfilms No. 8004982)

Russell, R. K., Crimmings, A. M., & Lent, R. W. (1984). Counselor training and supervision: Theory and research. In S. D. Brown & R. W. Lent (Eds.), *Handbook of counseling psychology* (pp. 625-681). New York: Wiley.

Sansbury, D. L. (1982). Developmental supervision from a skills perspective. *The Counseling Psychologist, 10*(1), 53-57.

Schmidt, J. P. (1979). Psychotherapy supervision: A cognitive-behavioral model. *Professional Psychology, 10,* 278-284.

Scofield, M. E. (with assistance of B. Butch, L. Montayne, & E. Butcher). (1981). *Written treatment planning simulation in mental health.* University Park, PA: Pennsylvania State University.

Searles, H. F. (1955). The informational value of the supervisor's emotional experiences. *Psychiatry, 18,* 135-146.

Slovenko, R. (1980). Legal issues in psychotherapy supervision. In A. K. Hess (Ed.), *Psychotherapy supervision: Theory, research and practice* (pp. 453-473). New York: Wiley.

Smith, H. D. (1984). Moment to moment counseling process feedback using a dual channel audiotape recording. *Counselor Education and Supervision, 23,* 346-349.

Smith, J. P., Jr. (1976). Supervisor behavior and supervisor expectations (Doctoral dissertation, University of Missouri—Columbia, 1975). *Dissertation Abstracts International, 36,* 6489A-6490A. (University Microfilms No. 76-7551)

Spice, C. G., Jr., & Spice, W. H. (1976). A triadic method of supervision in the training of counselors and counseling supervisors. *Counselor Education and Supervision, 15,* 251-258.

Stadler, H. (Ed.). (1986). Professional ethics [Special issue]. *Journal of Counseling and Development, 64*(5).

Stenack, R. J., & Dye, H. A. (1982). Behavioral descriptions of counseling supervision roles. *Counselor Education and Supervision, 21,* 295-304.

Stenack, R. J., & Dye, H. A. (1983). Practicum supervision roles: Effects on supervisee statements. *Counselor Education and Supervision, 23,* 157-168.

Stoltenberg, C. (1981). Approaching supervision from a developmental perspective: The counselor-complexity model. *Journal of Counseling Psychology, 28,* 59-65.

Stoltenberg, C. D., Solomon, G. S., & Ogden, L. (1986). Comparing supervisee and supervisor initial perceptions of supervision: Do they agree? *The Clinical Supervisor, 4*(3), 53-61.

Strosahl, K., & Jacobson, N. S. (1986). Training and supervision of behavior therapists. *The Clinical Supervisor, 4*(1-2), 183-206.

Strupp, H. H. (1981). *Vanderbilt Psychotherapy Process Scales (VPPS): Rater manual* (rev. ed.). Unpublished manuscript, Vanderbilt University, Nashville.

Styczynski, L. E. (1980). The transition from supervisee to supervisor. In A. K. Hess (Ed.), *Psychotherapy supervision: Theory, research and practice* (pp. 29-40). New York: Wiley.

Tennyson, W. W., & Strom, S. M. (1986). Beyond professional standards: Developing responsibleness. *Journal of Counseling and Development, 64,* 298-302.

Tentoni, S. C., & Robb, G. P. (1977). Improving the counseling program through immediate radio feedback. *College Student Journal, 12,* 279-283.

Trent, P. J., & Galassi, J. P. (1986, August). Evaluating supervision effectiveness. In J. P. Galassi (Chair), *Unresolved issues in counseling supervision.* Symposium conducted at the meeting of the American Psychological Association, Washington, DC.

Turock, A. (1980). Trainer feedback: A method for teaching interpersonal skills. *Counselor Education and Supervision, 19,* 216-222.

Tyler, J. D., & Weaver, S. H. (1981). Evaluating the clinical supervisee: A survey of practices in graduate training programs. *Professional Psychology, 12,* 434-437.

Upchurch, D. W. (1985). Ethical standards and the supervisory process. *Counselor Education and Supervision, 25,* 90-98.

Van Hoose, W., & Kottler, J. (1977). *Ethical and legal issues in counseling and psychotherapy.* San Francisco, CA: Jossey-Bass.

Walker, R. G. (1977). Short term psychotherapy with hospitalized schizophrenic patients. *Acta Psychiatrica Neurologica Scandinavia, 35,* 34-56.

Ward, D. E. (1984). Termination of individual counseling: Concepts and strategies. *Journal of Counseling and Development, 63,* 21-25.

Ward, L. G. (1986, August). Behavioral correlates of three dimensions of supervisory style. In M. L. Friedlander (Chair), *Innovative perspectives on the supervisory process.* Symposium conducted at the meeting of the American Psychological Association, Washington, DC.

Wasik, B. H., & Fishbein, J. E. (1982). Problem solving: A model for supervision in professional psychology. *Professional Psychology, 13,* 559-564.

Watson, D. K. (1973). Differential supervision. *Social Work, 18,* 80-88.

Weiner, I. B., & Kaplan, R. G. (1980). From classroom to clinic: Supervising the first psychotherapy client. In A. K. Hess (Ed.), *Psychotherapy supervision: Theory, research and practice* (pp. 41-50). New York: Wiley.

Wessler, R. L., & Ellis, A. (1980). Supervision in rational-emotive therapy. In A. K. Hess (Ed.), *Psychotherapy supervision: Theory, research and practice* (pp. 181-191). New York: Wiley.

Wessler, R. L., & Ellis, A. (1983). Supervision in counseling: Rational-emotive therapy. *The Counseling Psychologist, 11*(1), 43-49.

Wilbur, M. P., Roberts-Wilbur, J., Hart, G. M., & Betz, R. L. (1986). Structured group supervision: Integrating supervision models and group modalities. Unpublished manuscript.

Wiley, M. L., & Ray, P. B. (1986). Counseling supervision by developmental level. *Journal of Counseling Psychology, 33,* 439-445.

Williams, G. T., Yager, G. G., Woolum, S., Smaby, M. H., Sandor, D., & Woodward, D. (1985, November). The utilization of supervisory self-disclosure. Presentation at the meeting of the North Central Association for Counselor Education and Supervision, Chicago, IL.

Worthington, E. L., Jr. (1984). Empirical investigation of supervision of counselors as they gain experience. *Journal of Counseling Psychology, 31,* 63-75.

Worthington, E. L., Jr., & Roehlke, H. J. (1979). Effective supervision as perceived by beginning counselors-in-training. *Journal of Counseling Psychology, 26,* 64-73.

Worthington, E. L., Jr., & Stern, A. (1985). Effects of supervisor and supervisee degree level and gender on the supervisory relationship. *Journal of Counseling Psychology, 32,* 252-262.

Yager, G. G., & Beck, T. D. (1985). Beginning practicum: It only hurt until I laughed! *Counselor Education and Supervision, 25,* 149-157.

Yogev, S. (1982). An eclectic model of supervision: A developmental sequence for beginning psychotherapy students. *Professional Psychology, 13,* 236-243.

Zucker, P. J., & Worthington, E. L., Jr. (1986). Supervision of interns and postdoctoral applicants for licensure in university counseling centers. *Journal of Counseling Psychology, 33,* 87-89.